BASIC BIBLE
DOCTRINES

OF THE
CHRISTIAN FAITH

WHERE ARE THE DEAD?

Edward D. Andrews

WHERE ARE THE DEAD?

Basic Bible Doctrines of the Christian Faith

Edward D. Andrews

Christian Publishing House
Professional Christian Publishing of the Good News

Write support@christianpublishers.org

ISBN-13: **978-0692611128**

ISBN-10: **0692611126**

Christian Publishing House

Cambridge, Ohio

WHERE ARE THE DEAD? Basic Bible Doctrines of the Christian Faith

INTRODUCTION Why Do We Grow Old and Die?

In short, it was God's intention that his first couple, Adam and Eve, were to procreate, and cultivate the Garden of Eden until it covered the entire earth, filled with humans worshipping him. – Genesis 1:28

If the first couple had not rebelled, they and their offspring could have lived forever. – Genesis 2:15-17

One of the angels in heaven (who became Satan), abused his free will (Jam. 1:14-15). He chose to rebel against God, using a lowly serpent to contribute to Adam and Eve abusing their free will, and disobeying God, believing they did not need him, and could walk on their own. – Genesis 3:1-6; Job 1-2.

God removed the rebellious Adam and Eve from the Garden of Eden (Gen 3:23-24) The first human couple had children, but they all grew old and eventually died. (Gens 3:19; Rom. 5:12), just as the animals died. – Ecclesiastes 3:18-20

This battle for the mind began with Adam and Eve. You will likely remember that God laid only one restriction upon the first human couple, "but of the tree of the knowledge of good and evil you shall not eat, for in the day that you eat of it you shall surely die." (Gen. 2:17, ESV) Adam must have gone over this restriction with his new wife often and very well as Eve had it memorized and took it more serious than is usually taught. Satan, as the serpent hanging from the tree, was very clever and ingenious in how he indirectly said, "Did God actually say, 'You shall not eat of any tree in the garden'?" (Gen. 3:1) The woman replied to the serpent, "We may eat of the fruit of the trees in the garden, but God said, 'You shall not eat of the fruit of the tree that is in the midst of the garden, neither shall you touch it, lest you die.'" – Genesis 3:2-3.

Notice how Eve, not only responded with the correct answer, but she was also very emphatic, going beyond the actual command, saying that they were to not only **not eat** from the tree, but they were **not to even touch it**. "You can be sure that you will not die," the serpent said to the woman. "God knows that when you eat the fruit of that tree, you will know things you have never known before. You will be able to tell the difference between good and evil. You be like God." (Gen 3:4-5) The woman made two mistakes at that moment, **(1)** she did not consult her head, Adam, and **(2)** she entertained, cultivated this misleading, slanderous information. "When the woman saw that the tree *was good* for food and that it *was* a delight to the eyes, and the tree was desirable to make *one* wise, then she took from its fruit and she ate. *Afterward* she gave *it* also to her husband with her, and he ate."--Genesis 3:6

Here Eve was deceived because she looked at the tree differently than she had before. Eve lost the battle for her mind based on this supposedly new set of "truths,"

(1) She would not die,

(2) the fruit of the tree would make her wise,

(3) She would be like God, independent, able to determine for herself what is good and what is bad, setting her own standard.

Now, this one tree looked no different from any of the other thousands of trees in the Garden of Eden. Yet Eve now says 'the fruit of the tree looked good, it was pleasing to look at.' The human eyes are the window to the human mind-heart, the seat of motivation. Eve, even though she was perfect, meaning that her natural desire was to do good, stumbled based on the principle that James gave his readers. "Each person is tempted when he is lured and enticed by his own desire. Then desire when it has conceived gives birth to sin, and sin when it is fully grown brings forth death." – James 1:14-15

We notice too that Satan was so crafty that he was able to deceive another perfect creature to go against the grain of her perfected leanings, and violate God's one prohibition, even though it had been so deeply ingrained in her. Eve was misled by misinformation and lies that were ingeniously presented in a very subtle, indirect way. Notice Paul's words to the first-century Corinthian congregation, "But I am afraid lest somehow, as the serpent deceived Eve by his craftiness, your minds may be led astray from the sincerity and the purity of devotion to Christ." Yes, Satan has misled Eve by his craftiness, leading her mind astray from what she knew to be true, getting her to accept the lie. – 2 Corinthians 11:3.

Later Bible texts establish Satan the Devil as the one using a serpent as his mouthpiece like a ventriloquist would a dummy. Anyway, take note that Satan contradicts the clear statement made by God to Adam in Genesis 2:17, "you will not surely die." Backing up a little, we see Satan asking an inferential question, "Did God actually say, 'You shall not eat of any tree in the garden'?" First, he is overstating what he knows to be true, not "any tree," just one tree. Second, Satan is inferring, 'I can't believe that God would say . . . how dare he say such.' Notice too that Eve has been told so thoroughly about the tree that she even goes beyond what Adam told her, not just that you 'do not eat from it,' no, 'you do not even touch it!' Then, Satan out and out lied and slandered God as a liar, saying that 'they would not die.' To make matters much worse, he infers that God is withholding good from them, and by rebelling they would be better off, being like God, 'knowing good and bad.' This latter point is not knowledge of; it is the self-sovereignty of choosing good and bad for oneself, and act of rebellion for created creatures. What was symbolized by the tree is well expressed in a footnote on Genesis 2:17, in The Jerusalem Bible (1966):

This knowledge is a privilege which God reserves to himself and which man, by sinning, is to lay hands on, **3:5, 22**. Hence it does not mean omniscience, which fallen man does not possess; nor is it moral discrimination, for unfallen man already had it and God could not refuse it to a rational being. It is the power of deciding for himself what is good and what is evil and of acting accordingly, a claim to complete moral independence by which man refuses to recognise his status as a created being. The first sin was an attack on God's sovereignty, a sin of pride.

The Issues at Hand

(1) Satan called God a liar and said he was not to be trusted, as to the life or death issue.

(2) Satan's challenge, therefore, took into question the right and legitimacy of God's rightful place as the Universal Sovereign.

(3) Satan also suggested that people would remain obedient to God only as long as their submitting to God was to their benefit.

(4) Satan all but said that humankind was able to walk on his own, there being no need for dependence on God.

(5) Satan argued that man could be like God, choosing for himself what is right and wrong.

(6) Satan claimed that God's way of ruling was not in the best interests of humans, and they could do better without God.

Job 1:6-11 English Standard Version (ESV)

⁶ Now there was a day when the sons of God came to present themselves before the Lord, and Satan also came among them. ⁷ The Lord said to Satan, "From where have you come?" Satan answered the Lord and said, "From going to and fro on the earth, and from walking up and down on it." ⁸ And the Lord said to Satan, "Have you considered my servant Job, that there is none like him on the earth, a blameless and upright man, who fears God and turns away from evil?" ⁹ Then Satan answered the Lord and said, "<u>Does Job fear God for no reason</u>? ¹⁰ Have you not put a hedge around him and his house and all that he has, on every side? You have blessed the work of his hands, and his possessions have increased in the land. ¹¹ But <u>stretch out your hand and touch all that he has, and he will curse you to your face</u>."

Job 2:4-5 English Standard Version (ESV)

⁴ Then Satan answered the Lord and said, "Skin for skin! All that **a man** has he will give for his life. ⁵ But stretch out your hand and touch his bone and his flesh, and he will curse you to your face."

This general reference to "a man," as opposed to explicitly naming Job, is suggesting that all men [and women] will only obey God when things are good, but when the slightest difficulty arises, he will not obey. If you were put to the test, would you prove your love for your heavenly Father and show that you preferred His rule to that of any other?

Psalm 51:5 English Standard Version (ESV)	**Romans 5:12** English Standard Version (ESV)
⁵ Behold, I was brought forth in iniquity, and in sin did my mother conceive me.	¹² Therefore, just as sin came into the world through one man, and death through sin, and so death spread to all men because all sinned

God created both Adam and Eve perfect, with the outlook of living for eternity. However, he did give them free will, meaning they could have chosen to obey or disobey. He wanted them to obey him because of their love for him. They had the ability to love him even more fully than any imperfect human that has ever lived. Satan, the Devil succeeded in getting Adam to rebel through his love for Eve.

Adam was not deceived; he simply chose that his love was greater for Eve than it was for his Creator. Paul in 1 Timothy 2:14 is not shifting the blame on Eve; it is Adam, who was responsible for sin, old age and death entering the world of humankind. (Rom. 5:12, 19; 1 Cor. 15:22) Unlike Eve, he was not deceived by the lie that they would not die, or that God was withholding good from them, such as special knowledge. Both Adam and Eve intentionally and willfully went on a course of self-resolve, and rebellion against God. Adam's sin was far more severe than that of Eve. Moreover, it is his status as the head of Eve and the human race, which laid the full accountability at his feet. However, we must realize that Adam also fell in the battle for his mind. Satan likely observed the couple for some time and came to believe that he would choose Eve, the newer person to the Garden of Eden first. Further, Satan must have believed that Adam would selfishly desire Eve over his Creator. In the end, Satan won this first battle for the minds of Adam and Eve. – Genesis 2:17; 3:1-19; 5:3-5; compare Deuteronomy 32:4 and Revelation 12:9.

Satan got his rebellion, but he could not keep his worshipers alive. Sin began in the first human couple the moment Adam sinned, which meant any offspring would inherit that sin, i.e., missing the mark of perfection. Yes, Adam and Eve, once outside the Garden of Eden could only produce imperfect offspring, which inherited sin and death.

CHAPTER 1 Do We Have a Soul that Is Apart From Us?

Ministers, pastors, elders, overseers, leaders of churches have made many comments to those who have lost their loved one prematurely, in a car accident, natural disaster, war, and the like. They make such comments, such as, "While we grieve for the loss of Julie Sanford, we know she is the one in a better place, and now she truly knows what joy, peace, and happiness are, because she is with the Lord." If we attended the funerals of different churches, we would find similar messages being given to the family of the loved one, who has died. What all of these message have in common are, the belief in survival after death.

Some teach that the human soul is deathless and cannot die. These ones believe that we possess an immortal soul, which is death proof. One commentator, J. Warner Wallace, in an article entitled (What Happens to Our Souls When We Die?), writes, "There is good reason to believe our afterlife experience begins the minute we close our eyes for the last time here on earth. For those of us who are believers, the instant our earthly bodies die our souls will be united with Jesus in the afterlife." He goes on to write, "Each of us will leave our earthly bodies in the grave and our disembodied souls will go immediately into the presence of God or into Hades.[1] Our destination is determined purely by our acceptance or rejection of God through our faith in Jesus Christ."[2]

Surviving Death

The belief in most of Christianity is that we have a soul, **not that** we are a soul, and the soul that we have does not die. In other words, they believe that a soul within us is death proof, deathless, cannot die, i.e., is immortal. They observe that when a human body dies, it eventually turns into dust, (Gen. 3:19) but some part of the human must survive the body, and it is invisible to humans, untouchable, which some call the "soul," while others call this immaterial part of man "spirit." In order to get the theological position, we will quote Dr. Elmer Towns at length, He is a co-founder, with Jerry Falwell, of Liberty University, is a college and seminary professor, and Dean of the School of Religion, and Dean of Liberty University Baptist Theological Seminary.

---

[1] For a discussion of Hades, i.e., hellfire, please see the following

WHAT IS HELL? Basic Bible Doctrines of the Christian Faith by Edward D. Andrews

http://www.christianpublishers.org/apps/webstore/products/show/5346167

[2] http://coldcasechristianity.com/2014/what-happens-to-our-souls-when-we-die/

Theologians often debate the question of whether man is a two-part being (dichotomy) or a three-part being (trichotomy). Some verses seem to teach that man consists only of a body and soul, while others apparently teach a third aspect to man, the spirit. Sometimes the Bible seems to use the terms "soul" and "spirit" interchangeably, yet at other times a distinction between the two is more clearly made. Part of the problem is solved when we study the verses more closely and realize there are actually two ways to look at man. When we consider the nature or makeup of man, he is a two-part being. He consists of both material (the body) and the immaterial (the soul). In activity or function, however, the body, soul, and spirit of man each has a function. The distinction and similarity of the soul and spirit can be seen in a biblical discussion of the Word of God.

"For the word of God is quick, and powerful, and sharper than any two edged sword, piercing even to the dividing asunder of soul and spirit, and of the joints and marrow, and is a discerner of the thoughts and intents of the heart" (Heb. 4:12). The writer makes an interesting parallel. The joints and marrow are different in function, yet both are similar in that they are part of the bone structure of man. Thoughts and interests are also two distinct mental activities, yet they are similar in that they are activities of the mind. So the soul and spirit are distinct in function yet both are similar in immaterial composition. The writer is drawing five distinctions between things we may class together because of their similarity.

Soul. The Bible makes a clear distinction between the body and soul (Isa. 10:18). The term is used in the Bible to identify something that cannot be defined materially. The soul is that part of us that is life. At the creation of Adam, God "breathed into his nostrils the breath of life; and man became a living soul" (Gen. 2:7). Man did not have a soul but he became a soul, and the life-principle was the breath (Hebrew ruah: spirit) of God. As a result, we say when man no longer has breath that he is dead. When Rachel died in childbirth, the Bible described it "as her soul was in departing, (for she died)" (Gen. 35:18). In the Old Testament, the word "soul" is used to speak of the whole person (Song of Sol. 1:7).

Spirit. A further consideration of the immaterial side of man will reveal additional aspects of truth in examining the spirit of man. The term "spirit" is sometimes used in Scripture to speak of the mind (Gen. 8:1) or breath (1 Thess. 2:8).

That part of man that survives death is called the "spirit" in the Bible. When Stephen was stoned to death, the Bible identifies his spirit as departing the body when his life ended. "And they stoned Stephen, calling upon God, and saying, Lord Jesus, receive my spirit" (Acts 7:59). This principle is seen in the biblical definition of death. "For as the body without the spirit is dead, so faith without works is dead also" (James 2:28).

Relationship between the soul and spirit. The "soul" and "spirit" sometimes appear to be used interchangeably in Scripture (Gen. 41:8, and Ps. 42:6; John 12:27 and 13:21), because they both refer to the life-principle. We do not say man is a spirit, but that he has a spirit. On the other hand, we say man is a soul. The soul seems to be related to man's earthly life while the spirit relates to

man's heavenly life. The knowledge of God is received by man's spirit (1 Cor. 2:2–16) and interprets it for the total man. It is this spirit in man that is related to the higher things in man. The spirit of man is definitely related to the conversion experience. The apostle Paul acknowledged "The Spirit itself [the Holy Spirit] beareth witness with our spirit, that we are the children of God" (Rom. 8:16).

Man is a unity. Man is the spiritual link between the life of God and the physical life of this planet. Man is a twofold being, possessing a dual nature in unity; a dual nature because he is spiritual and he is physical. At times these two natures seem separate but they operate as one. Man has one personality, but possesses two natures that interact on each other. First, man's physical body is regulated by the material universe–he must eat, sleep, breathe, and live in dependence upon the earth. Man's body is an essential part of his constitution, so much so that he would not be man without a body. But in the second place, man is immaterial. This is the life of God that entered man when God breathed into him and he became a living soul. Man became immortal and will live forever because God, his source, is eternal. Since man was made in the image of God who created all things, man has creative abilities, to rule the physical earth.

Man with his dual nature is a unity. The material receives direction by the immaterial, and man's spiritual nature grows in harmony with physical well-being. God created man as a well-balanced unity. Those who harm their body sear their personality.

Sin entered God's perfect world as a foreign element and violated divine law. As a result, man was ruined spiritually and will die physically. God's purpose was thwarted and man's constitution was affected. The only thing that can restore his spiritual condition is the grace of God through the message of the gospel. Man's spiritual rebirth also guarantees for him a resurrected body that will again be made like his Maker.[3]

We would agree with some of Towns' point, but would also disagree with much. We will not take the time to refute systematically what he has written, we will just deal with what the Bible really teaches, and that will do it for us. Before delving into what the Bible really teaches, we will comment on one thing that Towns said, "God's purpose was thwarted." He is talking about God's intended purposes for man, (1) that he procreate with Eve and fill the earth with perfect humans, (2) that he cultivated the Garden of Eden until we would have had a paradise earth, (3) that he care for the animals. Now, are we to believe that Satan could actually thwart God's intended purpose?

THWART DEFINED: to prevent somebody or somebody's plan from being successful

Why not say that Satan sidetracked God purpose at best. If God had a purpose for man, are we to believe that one little act of Satan and Adam prevented him from seeing that purpose accomplished? God's purpose will be successfully accomplished through Jesus Christ. Satan merely delayed the inevitable fulfillment of God's will and purpose.

---

[3] Towns, Elmer (2011-10-30). AMG Concise Bible Doctrines (AMG Concise Series) (Kindle Locations 3584-3630). AMG Publishers. Kindle Edition.

The Human Soul

Let us turn to *A Hebrew and English Lexicon of the Old Testament*, based on the Lexicon of William Gesenius and edited by three clergymen, Drs. Brown, Driver and Briggs, in its corrected edition of 1952. On page 659, under the Hebrew word *Néfesh*, this Lexicon is honest enough to make this admission, in column two: "2. The *néfesh* becomes a living being; by God's breathing *neshamáth hhayím* into the nostrils of its *basár*; of man Genesis 2:7; by implication of animals also Genesis 2:19; so Psalm 104:29, 30, compare 66:9; man is *néfesh hhayáh*, a living, breathing being Genesis 2:7; elsewhere *néfesh hhayáh* always of animals Genesis 1:20, 24, 30; 9:12, 15, 16; Ezekiel 47:9; . . . 3. The *néfesh* . . . is specifically: a. a living being whose life resides in the blood . . . (hence sacrificial use of blood, and its prohibition in other uses; . . .) . . . c. *Néfesh* is used for life itself 171 times, of animals Proverbs 12:10, and of man Genesis 49:3c . . . "[4]

let us turn also to the *Lexicon for the Old Testament Books*, by L. Koehler and W. Baumgartner, in its edition of 1953, which gives definitions in both German and English. On page 627 of its Volume 2, this Lexicon says, under *Néfesh*: "*the breathing substance, making man and*

---

[4] In the above quotation the Hebrew words *neshamáth hhayím* mean "the breath of life." *Basár* means "flesh," and *néfesh hhayáh* means "a living soul," whether applied to animal or to man.

animal living beings Genesis 1:20, *the soul* (*strictly different from the Greek notion of soul*) *the seat of which is the blood* Genesis 9:4f; Leviticus 17:11; Deuteronomy 12:23 (249 times): 3. *néfesh hhayáh living being;* Genesis 1:20, 24 (= *animals*) 2:19 . . . 2:7; 9:10, 16. . . . 4. *soul = living being, individual, person* . . . *who kills a person* Numbers 31:19, . . . *destroy lives, persons* Ezekiel 22:27; . . . 7. *Néfesh breath = life* (282 times) . . . " And on page 628, column 1: "*Néfesh a dead one* (has developed from *a person*) Leviticus 21:1; Numbers 6:11; 9:10; Leviticus 22:4; Haggai 2:13; Numbers 5:2; 9:6f; 19:11, 13 . . . "

Many have wondered what happens to the soul after death. Do humans have a soul that is apart from them? What is the soul? Is the soul, some invisible force within us, which survives after death? While this seems farfetched to some, many believe this to be true. Many have heard the claims on television, in book and magazines, about those, who claim they have had so-called life-after-death experiences. Here is a question for you as a reader, before we look at the first Bile verse, 'Does the soul breathe to stay alive?' Likely, many would answer "no" to that question. Let us see what the Bible says.

A Soul Breathes

Genesis 2:7 American Standard Version (ASV)

⁷ And Jehovah God formed man of the dust of the ground, and breathed into his nostrils the breath of life; and man **became a living soul**.

The Christian apostle Paul, writer of fourteen books of the Bible, supports Moses' writings, saying, "So also it is written: 'The first man Adam became a living soul' … The first man was from the earth, a man of dust." (1 Cor. 15:45, 47, *UASV*)

Human soul = body **[dust of the ground]** + active life force **("spirit") [Hebrew, *ruach*]** within the trillions of human cells that make up the human body **+** breath of life [Hebrew, *neshamah*] that sustains the life force from God.

Genesis 2:7 tells us that God formed man out of the "dust of the ground." In other words, he was formed from the elements of the soil. This body needed life and so God caused the trillions of cells in his body to come to life, giving him the force of life. *Ruach* "spirit" is the active life force that Adam now possessed. However, for this life force to continue to feed these trillions of cells, there needed to be oxygen, sustained by the breathing. Therefore, we all know what God did next: he "breathed into his nostrils the breath [*neshamah*] of life." At this point, Adam's lungs would sustain the breathing the life force into those body cells.

If we are to understand fully what the "soul" is, we must investigate what the Hebrew and Greek words mean. The Hebrew word translated "soul" is *nephesh*. What does "nephesh" mean? The *Holman Illustrated Bible Dictionary* says,

> In the Hebrew OT, the word generally translated "soul" is *nephesh*. The word

occurs over 750 times, and it means primarily "life" or "possessing life." It is used of both animals (Gen. 9:12; Ezek. 47:9) and humans (Gen. 2:7). The word sometimes indicates the whole person, as for instance in Gen. 2:7 where God breathes breath (*neshamah*) into the dust and thus makes a "soul" (*nephesh*). A similar usage is found in Gen. 12:5 where Abram takes all the "souls" (persons) who were with him in Haran and moves on to Canaan. Similarly in Num. 6:6 it is used as a synonym for the body—the Nazirite is not to go near a dead *nephesh* (Lev. 7:21; Hag. 2:13). (Brand, Draper and Archie 2003, 1523)

Soul as "a living creature"

The American Standard Version has our literal rendering of *nephesh* at Genesis 2:7, "and man became **a** living **soul**." The English Standard Version offers an interpretation of *nephesh*, "and the man became **a** living **creature**." (LEB same) The Holman Christian Standard Bible offers an interpretation of *nephesh*, "and the man became **a** living **being**." (NASB same) You will notice that Genesis 2:7 makes it all too clear that Adam was not given a soul, he does not have a soul, but that he **became** a living soul, i.e., a living creature, a living being. Therefore, the "soul" is the person, the creature, the being, not what we have. When we look at the Hebrew Old Testament using a literal rendering, this is born out.

Leviticus 5:1 New American Standard Bible (NASB)

5 'Now **if a** person [*nephesh*, **soul**] **sins** after he hears a public adjuration *to testify* when he is a witness, whether he has seen or *otherwise* known, if he does not tell *it*, then he will bear his guilt.

Leviticus 23:30 New American Standard Bible (NASB)

30 As for **any** person [*nephesh*, **soul**] **who does any work** on this same day, that person I will destroy from among his people.

Deuteronomy 24:7 Lexham English Bible (LEB)

7 "If a man is *caught* **kidnapping** somebody [*nephesh*, **a soul**][5] from *among* his countrymen, the *Israelites*, and he treats him as a slave or he sells him, then that kidnapper shall die, and *so* you shall purge the evil *from among you*.

Judges 16:16 New American Standard Bible (NASB)

16 It came about when she pressed him daily with her words and urged him, that his **soul was annoyed** to death.

---

[5] Lit In case a man is found *kidnapping a soul* of his brothers of the sons of Israel

Job 19:2 Updated American Standard Version (UASV)

² How long will you **torment my soul**, And break me in pieces with words?

Psalm 119:28 New American Standard Bible (NASB)

²⁸ My **soul weeps** because of grief; Strengthen me according to Your word.

We notice here in the above verses that a soul sins, a soul works, a soul can be kidnapped, a soul can get annoyed, a soul can be tormented, and a soul can weep. These things happened to persons, to creatures, to beings, not inanimate objects within the human body, which is supposed lives on after death. *The Holman Illustrated Bible Dictionary* says,

> **New Testament** Greek word *psuche* carries many of the same meanings as the Hebrew *nephesh*. Often the soul is equated with the total person. Romans 13:1 says, "Everyone [soul] must submit to the governing authorities" equating "soul" (one) with "person" (cp. Acts 2:41; 3:23). There will be "affliction and distress for every human being [soul] who does evil, first to the Jew, and also to the Greek" (Rom. 2:9 HCSB). Soul in the NT also indicates the emotions or passions: "But the Jews who refused to believe stirred up and poisoned the minds [*psuche*] of the Gentiles against the brothers" (Acts

14:2 HCSB). In John 10:24 the Jews asked Jesus, "How long are You going to keep us [our souls] in suspense?" Jesus also told the disciples that they should love God with all of their souls (Mark 12:30), indicating something of the energy and passion that ought to go into loving Him. (Brand, Draper and Archie 2003, 1523)

When we look at the Greek New Testament using a literal rendering, "soul," the basic idea inherent in the word as the Bible writers used it, namely, that it is a living person, a living creature, or a living being; or, the life that a person or an animal has as a soul.

John 12:27 New American Standard Bible (NASB)

[27] "Now **My soul has become troubled**; and what shall I say, 'Father, save Me from this hour'? But for this purpose I came to this hour.

Acts 2:43 American Standard Version (ASV)

[43] And **fear came upon every soul**: and many wonders and signs were done through the apostles.

Romans 13:1 New American Standard Bible (NASB)

13 Every person [*psuche*, **soul**] is **to be in subjection** to the governing authorities. For there is no authority except from God, and those which exist are established by God.

1 Thessalonians 5:14 Lexham English Bible (LEB)

¹⁴ And we urge you, brothers, admonish the disorderly, console the **discouraged** [oligo*psuche*, literally "those of little **soul**," i.e., "discouraged."], help the sick, be patient toward all *people*.

1 Peter 3:20 New American Standard Bible (NASB)

²⁰ who once were disobedient, when the patience of God kept waiting in the days of Noah, during the construction of the ark, in which a few, that is, eight persons [*psuchai*, **souls**], were brought safely through *the* water.

We notice here in the above verses that a soul can become troubled, fear can come upon a soul, a soul is to be in subjection to the governmental authorities, a soul can get discouraged, and souls can be delivered through a flood. These things happen to a person, a creature, a being, not an inanimate object within the human body, which supposed lives on after death. We note to from our quote of *The Holman Illustrated Bible Dictionary*, animals are "souls" too.

Genesis 1:24 American Standard Version (ASV)	**Numbers 31:28** American Standard Version (ASV)
²⁴ And God said, Let the earth bring forth living creatures [*nephesh*, soul] after their kind, cattle,	²⁸ And levy a tribute unto Jehovah of the men of war that went

and creeping things, and beasts of the earth after their kind: and it was so.	out to battle: one soul of five hundred, both of the persons, and of the oxen, and of the asses, and of the flocks:

Soul as the Life of the Creature

"Soul" is used in Scripture as a reference to the life that a living person, a living creature, a living animal has. This does not negate what we learned in the above. We are living "souls," i.e., living persons. It does not change a thing to use "soul" in the sense of our possessing "life." Below are a few examples.

Exodus 4:19 American Standard Version (ASV)

¹⁹ And Jehovah said to Moses in Midian, "Go, return into Egypt, for all the men are dead who sought your life [*nephesh*, **soul**]."⁶

Joshua 9:24 American Standard Version (ASV)

²⁴ And they answered Joshua, and said, Because it was certainly told thy servants, how that Jehovah your God commanded his servant Moses to give you all the land, and to destroy all the inhabitants of the land from before you; therefore we feared greatly for our lives [*nephesh*, **souls**] because of you, and have done this thing.

---

⁶ Lit. all the men who were **seeking your soul** are dead.

2 Kings 7:7 American Standard Version (ASV)

7 Wherefore they arose and fled in the twilight, and left their tents, and their horses, and their asses, even the camp as it was, and fled for their life [*nephesh*, soul].

Proverbs 12:10 American Standard Version (ASV)

10 A righteous man regards the life [*nephesh*, soul] of his beast; But the tender mercies of the wicked are cruel.

Matthew 20:28 American Standard Version (ASV)

28 even as the Son of man came not to be ministered to, but to minister, and to give his life [*psuche*, soul] a ransom for many.

Philippians 2:30 New American Standard Bible (NASB)

30 because he came close to death for the work of Christ, risking his life [*psuche*, soul] to complete what was deficient in your service to me.

Now, we do not want to misrepresent the *Holman Illustrated Bible Dictionary*, by quoting two paragraphs, where this author would agree, and not go on to the next paragraph, where they would disagree with this author. There are two positions, when it comes to the biblical position of the body and the soul. **We would <u>disagree</u>** with the first, which is "**holistic dualism**—that there is a difference between body and soul, but the two are

31

linked together by God such that humans are not complete when the two are separated." Our position that **we would agree** with, would be the second, which is the "**monistic view** that the soul is not separable from the body at all. Nearly all who have held the second view have also believed that after death Christians 'go to sleep' and await the resurrection." (Bold mine, more on this below) *The Holman Illustrated Bible Dictionary* holds to the holistic dualism position, as they write,

> It is also the case that the NT speaks of the soul as something that is distinguishable from the physical existence of a person. Jesus made this point when He observed, "Don't fear those who kill the body but are not able to kill the soul; but rather, fear Him who is able to destroy both soul and body in hell" (Matt. 10:28 HCSB). James seems to have the same thing in mind when he concludes his letter, "He should know that whoever turns a sinner from the error of his way will save his life [soul] from death" (James 5:20 HCSB; cp. Rev. 6:9; 20:4). This may be the idea found in Mark 8:36, "For what does it benefit a man to gain the whole world yet lose his life [soul]?" (HCSB). Scripture clearly teaches that persons continue to exist consciously after physical death. Jesus pointed out that as the God of Abraham, Isaac, and Jacob, He is the God of the living. These still live, their souls having

returned to God (Eccles. 12:7). (Brand, Draper and Archie 2003, 1523)

We will take their texts one at a time, offering the text, and then offering a thought that will clarify what was meant by the author.

Matthew 10:28 Holman Christian Standard Bible (HCSB)

28 Don't fear those who kill the body but are not able to kill the soul; rather, fear Him who is able to destroy both soul and body in hell.[7]

What is meant by this is, man can kill the body alone, but he cannot kill "life," as in everlasting life. The prospect of life is in the hands of God alone. He can kill both the body, which is used to represent what we have here and now, but he can also kill any prospect that we have at everlasting life. Again, man can kill the body; he cannot kill the person for an eternity, as the hope of a resurrection is in hands of God.

James 5:20 Holman Christian Standard Bible (HCSB)

20 let him know that whoever turns a sinner from the error of his way will save his life **[soul]** from death and cover a multitude of sins.

---

[7] For a discussion of the hellfire doctrine, please see, **BASIC TEACHINGS OF THE BIBLE Life Questions Christians Ask Themselves and Others** by Andrews, Edward D. (Nov 28, 2013)

First, we should point out that, the 'life **[soul]** that is saved from death' is, not the one doing the helping, but rather, it is the sinner. Our works do not save us; we are saved by the loving-kindness of God, in offering his Son as a ransom sacrifice for all, who trust in that sacrifice. (Acts 4:12) The person who was saved was walking down the path of eternal death, from where there is no hope for eternal life. When the one Christian helped the sinner turn back from his error, by spreading love and counsel, as well as prayer, he helped this sinner stay on the path of life, eternal life, by way of the atonement sacrifice of Christ.

Mark 8:36 Holman Christian Standard Bible (HCSB)

[36] For what does it benefit a man to gain the whole world yet lose his life **[soul]**?

Here again, it is not referring to the person's life in this present imperfect age, but eternal life that is to come after Jesus brings the last enemy to nothing, death. We will deal with Ecclesiastes 12:7 below.

Can the Soul Die?

When we die, what happens to the soul? If you recall from above that the "soul" is the person, the being, the creature, i.e., us, and the **life** that we have. If you recall from above, the **Human soul** = body **[dust of the ground]** + active life force **("spirit") [Hebrew, *ruach*]** within the trillions of human cells which make up the human body **+** breath of life [Hebrew, *neshamah*] that sustains the life force from God. In other words, the "soul" is we as a whole, everything that we are, so the soul or we humans can die. Let us look at a few verses, which make that all too clear.

Ecclesiastes 3:19-20 New American Standard Bible (NASB)

¹⁹ For the fate of the sons of men **[humans or people]** and the fate of beasts is the same. As one dies so dies the other; indeed, they all have the same breath and there is no advantage for man over beast, for all is vanity. ²⁰ All go to the same place. All came from the dust and all return to the dust.

In other words, when we breathe our last breath, our cells begin to die. Death is the ending of all vital functions or processes in an organism or cell. When our heart stops beating, our blood is no longer circulating, carrying nourishment and oxygen (by breathing) to the trillions of cells in our body; we are what are termed, clinically dead. However, somatic death has yet to occur, meaning we can be revived, after many minutes of being clinically dead, if the heart and lungs can be restarted again, which gives the cells the oxygen they need.

After about three minutes of clinical death, the brain cells begin to die, meaning the chances of reviving the person is less likely as each second passes. We know that it is vital that the breathing and blood flow be maintained for the life force (*ruach chaiyim*) in the cells. Nevertheless, it is not the lack of breathing or the failure of the heart beating alone, but rather the active life force **("spirit") [Hebrew, ruach]** within the trillions of human cells which make up the human body **+** breath of life [Hebrew, *neshamah*] that sustains the life force from God.

Psalm 104:29 (ESV)	Psalm 146:4 (ESV)	Ecclesiastes 8:8 (ESV)
29 When you hide your face, they are dismayed; when you take away their breath, they die and return to their dust.	4 When his breath departs, he returns to the earth; on that very day his plans perish.	8 No man has power to retain the spirit, or power over the day of death. There is no discharge from war, nor will wickedness deliver those who are given to it.

Again, …

Ezekiel 18:4 (ESV)	Leviticus 21:1 (ASV)	Numbers 6:6 (ASV)
4 Behold, all souls are mine; the soul of the father as well as the soul of the son is mine: the	21 And Jehovah said to Moses, Speak to the priests, the sons of Aaron, and say	6 All the days that he separates himself unto Jehovah he shall not come

soul who sins shall die.	to them, There shall none defile himself for the dead **[Or "for a soul."]** among his people;	near to a dead body **[Or "soul."]**.

Again, the death of a "soul" means the death of a person …

1 Kings 19:4 (ASV)	Jonah 4:8 (ASV)	Mark 3:4 (ASV)
4 But he himself went a day's journey into the wilderness, and came and sat down under a juniper-tree: and he requested for himself that he **[Or "his soul.]** "might die, and said, It is enough; now, O Jehovah, take away my life [soul]; for I am not better than my fathers.	8 And it came to pass, when the sun arose, that God prepared a sultry east wind; and the sun beat upon the head of Jonah, that he fainted, and requested for himself that he might die **[Or "that his soul might die."]**, and said, It is better for me to die than to live.	4 And he said to them, Is it lawful on the sabbath day to do good, or to do harm? to save a life **[Or "soul."]**, or to kill? But they held their peace.

As you can see from the above texts, a "soul," or person can die. However, how are we to understand those texts that say the "soul" went out of a person, or came back into a person?

Soul Departing and Soul Coming into a Person

Genesis 35:18 English Standard Version (ESV)

18 And as her soul was departing (for she was dying), she called his name Ben-oni; but his father called him Benjamin.

Are we to understand from this that Rachel had some inner being, a soul, which departed from her at death? No. You will recall from the texts from above that the term "soul" can also be used in reference to the life one has. Thus, this is a reference to her life that she had leaving her. Note the *Lexham English Bible*, "And it happened *that* when **her _life_ was departing** (for she was dying), she called his name Ben-Oni. But his father called him Benjamin." (Bold and underline is mine) Therefore, it was her "life" that she had, which departed from her, not some inner being.

1 Kings 17:22 American Standard Version (ASV)

22 And Jehovah listened to the voice of Elijah; and the soul of the child came into him again, and he revived.

Here again, the word "soul" is the "life" that someone has. The *New American Standard Bible* reads, "The **life** of the child returned to him and he revived." The *Lexham English Bible* reads, "The **life** of the child returned within him, and he lived." The *Holman Christian Standard Bible* reads, "The boy's **life** returned to him, and he lived." (Bold is mine)

John 11:11 (ESV)	**1 Kings 2:10** (ESV)
[11] After saying these things, he said to them, "Our friend Lazarus has fallen asleep, but I go to awaken him."	[10] Then David slept with his fathers and was buried in the city of David.

Notice that Lazarus' death is equated with being asleep in death, while King David is referred to as sleeping in death. This gives the reader a hope, as just as easily as you and I can awaken a person from sleep, Jesus is going to awaken people from death, a death like sleep. We are going to look at these verses a little differently that we have with the others. We will pause for a moment to see how a literal translation is best (which has already been demonstrated), with an interpretation in a footnote. Moreover, it is important that we read those footnotes. Otherwise, we can come to the wrong conclusions.

Souls Have Blood

As we know by now, the Bible's viewpoint is that the living human creature is the human soul. In addition, though, the Bible states that the human soul has blood.

Jeremiah 2:34 Updated American Standard Version (UASV)

34 Also on your skirts is found **the blood of the souls** of the innocent poor; you did not find them breaking in. But in spite of all these things,

God says,

Genesis 9:5 Updated American Standard Version (UASV)

5 Surely I will require **your blood of your souls**;[8] from every beast I will require it. From every beast[9] will I require it. And at the hand of man, even at the hand of every man's brother, will I require the **soul**[10] of man.[11]

The Creator himself shows us the level of dependence of the human soul upon the blood stream by saying,

---

[8] Or *your blood of your lives* (your lifeblood)

[9] Lit *from the hand of*

[10] Heb., *nephesh*, as in 2:7; Gr., *psuche*.

[11] The Creator of the heavens and the earth, Adam and Eve views blood as standing for life.

Leviticus 17:11 Updated American Standard Version (UASV)

[11] For the soul of the flesh is in the blood, and I have given it to you upon the altar to make atonement for your souls; for it is the blood that makes atonement by the soul.[12]

Leviticus 17:14 Updated American Standard Version (UASV)

[14] "For as for the soul of all flesh, its blood is *identified* with its soul. Therefore I said to the sons of Israel, 'You are not to eat the blood of any flesh, for the soul of all flesh is its blood; whoever eats it shall be cut off.'

Deuteronomy 12:23 Updated American Standard Version (UASV)

[23] Only be sure not to eat the blood, for **the blood is the soul**, and you shall not eat the soul with the flesh.

Souls can Eat Fat and Blood

Human souls can eat both blood and Fat, but God prohibited it. Nevertheless, the point is that human souls can eat fat and blood. All of the different points being made with these Scriptures are that the soul is the person, not some entity inside of us that goes to another realm somewhere when we die.

---

[12] i.e., atonement by the soul *in it*

41

Leviticus 7:25 Updated American Standard Version (UASV)

25 For whoever eats the fat of the animal from which an offering by fire is offered to Jehovah, even **the soul who eats** shall be cut off from his people.

Leviticus 7:27 Updated American Standard Version (UASV)

27 Any **soul who eats** any blood, that soul must be cut off from his people.'"

The human soul can also eat the dead animal souls. Thus, we see in this one verse that animals are souls as well and that if any Israelite violated certain parts of the Mosaic Law he would be cut off by expelling him or even executing. However, the text refers to the soul being cut off.

Leviticus 17:15 Updated American Standard Version (UASV)

15 And every **soul who eats** what dies of itself or what is torn by beasts, whether he is a native or a sojourner, shall wash his clothes and bathe himself in water and be unclean until the evening; then he shall be clean.

Human Souls Desire to Eat Meet

Deuteronomy 12:20 Updated American Standard Version (UASV)

20 "When Jehovah your God enlarges your territory, as he has promised you, and you say, 'I will eat meat,' because your soul craves to eat meat, your soul may eat meat whenever you desire.

Deuteronomy 23:24 Updated American Standard Version (UASV)

24 "When you enter your neighbor's vineyard, then you may eat grapes until you satisfy your soul, but you shall not put any in your basket.

Proverbs 27:7 Updated American Standard Version (UASV)

7 A soul who is full loathes honey,
but to the soul who is hungry everything bitter is sweet.

The reader may wonder why this author is using a translation that is not even fully complete at the time of penning this book. It is because the "so-called" literal translations (ESV, HCSB, even the NASB) are letting their readers down.

Leviticus 17:11 (ESV)	Leviticus 17:11 (HCSB)	Leviticus 17:11 (NASB)
11 For the life of the flesh is in the blood, and I have given it for you on the altar to make atonement for **your souls**, for it is the blood that makes	11 For the life of a creature is in the blood, and I have appointed it to you to make atonement on the altar for[a] your lives, since it is the	For the [a]life of the flesh is in the blood, and I have given it to you on the altar to make atonement for **your souls**; for it is the blood by

atonement by the life.	lifeblood that makes atonement. **Footnotes:** [a] Leviticus 17:11 Or *to ransom*	reason of the [b]life that makes atonement.' **Footnotes:** [a] Leviticus 17:11 Lit *soul* [b] Leviticus 17:11 Lit *soul*

Only the NASB, at least, places the literal rendering in the footnote, when it should be in the main text. Leviticus 17:11 is indicative of all the verses above. This has allowed the reader to see they are not getting what they were promised, i.e., a literal translation. We have shown the translations and their footnotes. We have only looked at the ESV, HCSB, and the NASB. First, *nephesh* "soul" or souls" appear three times in Leviticus 17:11. The NASB used the corresponding English "souls" once but does not stay faithful to their literal translation philosophy the other two times. However, unlike the others, they at least offer the reader a footnote, so he will know what was actually in the main text. The HCSB does not remain faithful to their claim of being literal one time out of the three, nor do they offer the reader a footnote. The ESV used the corresponding English "souls" once but does not stay faithful to their literal translation philosophy the other two times. Worse still, they **did not** offer the reader a footnote, so he will know what was actually in the main text.

Why should we be so the concerned over the literal rendering versus an interpretative rendering? Why should we be so worried over the necessity of being constant? One might ask. How can I know the truth about the Hebrew term *nephesh* (translated "soul" by the USAV) and the Greek term *psuche* (translated "soul" by the USAV)? If we look to the dynamic equivalent (interpretive) translations and the literal translations, we will discover that they use more than thirty English words when they translate *nephesh* and *psuche*. What English readers are not aware of, because most do not even add a footnote, which most English readers bypass anyway; there is just one Hebrew word and one Greek word behind all of those different English words.

We are not suggesting that the interpretation translation is incorrect, just inappropriate. Genesis 35:18 in the ESV says, "And as **her soul was departing** (for she was dying), she called his name Ben-oni; but his father called him Benjamin.)" First, notice that the ESV translators are not shy about using the rendering "soul" here, whereas they use an interpretive word in most other places, with no footnote. Why? Would it be because, to the average reader, Genesis 35:18 appears to support that we do have an immaterial part of humans that leaves when we die? Would it be that if we rendered *nephesh* and *psuche* as "soul" in all the other places, it would negate such an idea? Now, the interpretive translations here actually explain what is meant. These translations render the phrase "her soul was departing" as "her life was departing" (LEB), "With her last breath" (HCSB), and "her life went from her" (BBE). We can clearly see that no immaterial part of Rachel survived her body after her death. She was dead, awaiting a future resurrection.

Yes, we cannot fully understand what the Bible authors meant by their use of *nephesh* and *psuche*, if the translator is not consistent in his rendering of those terms. When a serious Bible reader has a translation that shows

(1) that we do not have a soul,

(2) but that we are souls,

(3) animals are souls,

(4) souls eat food,

(5) souls have blood,

(6) souls die,

(7) and dead bodies are even called souls,

they will come to understand that the Bible scholars who say the immortal soul concept **is not found** in God's Word but is found in Greek literature **are correct**, as opposed to those scholars, like Elmer Towns, who claim an immaterial part of the human is found within the Scriptures. Now, even though the dynamic equivalent translations are correct as to the meaning, it is clear that the literal translation consistently rendered, with the interpretive rendering in a footnote will give us a clear understand of the soul. Thus, let us take a few more moments contrasting the dynamic equivalent translation with the literal translation.

Dynamic Equivalent Translations Hide the Truth

1 Kings 2:10 Essentially Literal Translation (ASV, RSV, ESV, NASB)

And David slept with his fathers, and was buried in the city of David.

And David slept with his fathers, and was buried in the city of David.

Then David slept with his fathers and was buried in the city of David.

Then David slept with his fathers and was buried in the city of David.

1 Kings 2:10 Though-for-Thought Translation (GNB, CEV, NLT, MSG)

David died and was buried in David's City.

Then he died and was buried in Jerusalem.

Then David died and was buried with his ancestors in the City of David.

Then David joined his ancestors. He was buried in the City of David.

One could conclude that the thought-for-thought translations are conveying the idea in a more clear and immediate way, but is this really the case? There are three points that are missing from the thought-for-thought translation:

In the scriptures, "sleep" is used metaphorically as death, also inferring a temporary state where one will wake again, or be resurrected. That idea is lost in the thought-for-thought translation. (Ps 13:3; John 11:11-14; Ac 7:60; 1Co 7:39; 15:51; 1Th 4:13)

David's sleeping with or lying down with his father also conveys the idea of having closed his life and having found favor in God's eyes as did his forefathers.

When we leave out some of the words from the original, we also leave out the possibility of more meaning being drawn from the text. Missing is the word *shakab* ("to lie down" or "to sleep"), *'im* ("with") and 'ab in the plural ("forefathers").

Psalm 13:3 American Standard Version (ASV)

Consider *and* answer me, O Jehovah my God: Lighten mine eyes, lest I sleep the *sleep of* death

John 11:11-14 American Standard Version (ASV)

After saying these things, he said to them, "Our friend Lazarus is fallen asleep; but I go, that I may awake him out of sleep." The disciples therefore said to him, Lord, if he is fallen asleep, he will recover. Now Jesus had spoken of his death: but they thought that he spoke of taking rest in sleep. Then Jesus therefore said to them plainly, Lazarus is dead.

Acts 7:60 American Standard Version (ASV)

And he kneeled down, and cried with a loud voice, Lord, lay not this sin to their charge. And when he had said this, he fell asleep.

1 Corinthians 7:39 (Updated American Standard Version)

A wife is bound as long as her husband lives. But if her husband should sleep (*koimethe*) [in death], she is free to be married to whom she wishes, only in the Lord.[13]

1 Corinthians 15:51 American Standard Version (ASV)

Behold, I tell you a mystery: We all shall not sleep, but we shall all be changed,

1 Thessalonians 4:13 American Standard Version (ASV)

But we would not have you ignorant, brethren, concerning them that fall asleep; that ye sorrow not, even as the rest, who have no hope.

Those who argue for a though-for-thought translation will say the literal translation "slept" or "lay down" is no longer a way of expressing death

---

[13] The ASV, ESV, NASB, and other literal translation do not hold true to their literal translation philosophy here. This does not bode well in their claim that literal renderings are to be preferred. I am speaking primarily to the ESV translators, who make this claim in numerous books.

in the modern English-speaking world. While this may be true to some extent, the context of chapter two, verse 1: "when David was about to die" and the latter half of 2:10: "was buried in the city of David" really resolves that issue. Moreover, while the reader may have to meditate a little longer, or indulge him/herself in the culture of different Biblical times, they will not be deprived of the full potential that a verse has to convey. (*Translating Truth*, Grudem, Ryken, Collins, Polythress, & Winter, 2005, 21-22) Therefore, we offer a word of caution here. The dynamic equivalent can and does obscure things from the reader by overreaching in their translations.

His Spirit Goes Forth and He Returns to the Earth

Psalm 146:4 Young's Literal Translation (YLT)

⁴ His spirit goes forth; he returns to his earth, In that day have his thoughts perished.

Are we to understand that there is some spiritual being within us, which then departs from us at death? No, this is not the understanding, as the Psalmist next words were, "In that day have his thoughts perished," ("all his thinking ends," *NEB*). How, then, are we to understand this verse?

In the Hebrew Scriptures, we have *ruach*, and in the Greek New Testament, we have *pneuma*, both with the basic meaning "breath." This is why other translations read, "His breath goes forth."

Psalm 146:4 (ESV)	Psalm 146:4 (LEB)	Psalm 146:4 (HCSB)
⁴ When his **breath departs**, he returns to the earth; on that very day his plans perish.	⁴ His **breath departs**; he returns to his plot; on that day his plans perish.	⁴ When his **breath leaves** him, he returns to the ground; on that day his plans die.

You will notice this further clarified, when Moses informs us of what took place at the flood. However, we look at the literal translations first, followed by other literal translations that choose to define the use of the term "spirit." Note how we will use a footnote in the literal, and the others that chose to define.

Genesis 7:22 (NASB)	Genesis 7:22 (ASV)	Genesis 7:22 (YLT)
²² of all that was on the dry land, all in whose nostrils was the breath of the spirit of life **[breath of life]**, died.	²² all in whose nostrils was the breath of the spirit of life **[breath of life]**, of all that was on the dry land, died.	²² all in whose nostrils [is] breath of a living spirit **[breath of life]** -- of all that [is] in the dry land -- have died.

Other literal and semi-literal translations,

Genesis 7:22 (ESV)	Genesis 7:22 (LEB)	Genesis 7:22 (NRSV)
22 Everything on the dry land in whose nostrils was the breath of life **["a breath of spirit of life"]** died.	22 Everything in whose nostrils *was the breath of life* **["a breath of spirit of life"]**, among all that *was* on dry land, died.	22 everything on dry land in whose nostrils was the breath of life **["a breath of spirit of life"]** died.

Therefore, "*ruach*" and "pneuma," i.e., "spirit" can refer to the breath of life that is active within both human and animal creatures. Then how do we explain Ecclesiastes 12:7?

Ecclesiastes 12:7 English Standard Version (ESV)

7 and the dust returns to the earth as it was, and the spirit returns to God who gave it.

Are we to understand that a spiritual being within us, leaves us at death, and returns to God? No. We just learned that the "spirit" is the "breath of life," which sustains human and animal life. Once we lose our "breath of life," and are dead, the only hope of having it restored comes from God. Therefore, "the spirit returns to God," in that our only hope for living again, but this time for eternally, comes from God. It is only God, who can restore the "breath of life," which allows us to live again. Keep in mind too, this person was never in heaven with God, so the idea of him as a spirit person returning to God is not what is meant. How can he return to God, if he was never in heaven with God to begin with? Again, it is the "breath of life," which enables the person to live that returns to God, not literally, but in the sense of his having the power to restore it.

Ecclesiastes 12:7 (LEB)	**Ecclesiastes 12:7** (NRSV)
[7] And the dust returns to the earth as it was, and the breath returns to God who gave it.	[7] and the dust returns to the earth as it was, and the breath returns to God who gave it.

All conservative Christians would point to the Bible as the final authority on all doctrine. This is true of our understanding of the *soul* as well. In the Hebrew Old Testament, the Hebrew word *nephesh* (translated "soul" in the UASV) is found 754 times, first in Genesis 1:20. In the Greek New Testament, the Greek word *psuche* (translated "soul" in the UASV) is found by itself 102 times, first in Matthew 2:20. In each case, a literal translation, looking to give its readers what God had said, should render this Hebrew and Greek word "soul," with the interpretive rendering in the footnote. By doing this, the reader of the Bible will be able to see how the word "soul" is used within the whole of the inspired, inerrant Word of God.

CHAPTER 2 The Bible's Viewpoint of Death

Death is the end of all functions of life, namely, the opposite of life. (Deut. 30:15, 19) Within Scripture, the same Hebrew words of the Old Testament and Greek words of the New Testament are used with humans, animals, and plants. (Eccles. 3:19; 9:5; John 12:24; Jude 12; Rev. 16:3) However, as we have already learned in the above, the Bible shows the essential purpose of the blood in preserving life, stating, "The soul [life] of the flesh is in the blood." (Lev. 17:11, 14; Gen. 4:8-11; 9:3, 4) The Bible says,

Genesis 7:21-24 Updated American Standard Version (UASV)

21 All flesh that moved[14] on the earth perished, birds and cattle and beasts and every swarming thing that swarms[15] upon the earth, and all mankind; **22** of all that was on the dry land, all in whose nostrils was the breath of the spirit of life,[16] died. **23** Thus he blotted out every living thing that was on the face of the ground, man and animals and creeping things and birds of the heavens.[17] They

---

[14] Or *crept*

[15] Lit *all the swarming swarms*

[16] Literally "a breath of spirit of life" Heb., *'asher-boh´ ruach chaiyim´*. Here *ruach* means "animating force; spirit."

[17] Or "the sky"

54

were blotted out from the earth. Only Noah was left, and those who were with him in the ark. **24** The water prevailed upon the earth one hundred and fifty days.

Notice that the Bible says that both humans and animals died, i.e., perished. Literally, that means 'breathing out' the breath of life (Heb., *nishmath´ chaiyim´*). (Gen. 7:21, 22; see Gen. 2:7.) Moreover, the Bible shows when both human and animals suffer somatic death (Death of the entire body), where there is a loss of "a breath of spirit of life," i.e., the "animating force; spirit." (Heb., *ruach chaiyim´*)—Gen 6:17; 7:15, 22; Eccles. 3:19

What is death?

Under this heading, we will repeat what was penned earlier, as repetition for emphasis. It is recommended that you read these few Scriptures and paragraphs again. When we die, what happens to the soul? If you recall from above that the "soul" is the person, the being, the creature, i.e., us, and the **life** that we have. If you recall from above, the **Human soul** = body **[dust of the ground]** + active life force **("spirit") [Hebrew, *ruach*]** within the trillions of human cells which make up the human body **+** breath of life [Hebrew, *neshamah*] that sustains the life force from God. In other words, the "soul" is we as a whole, everything that we are, so the soul or we humans can die. Let us look at a few verses, which make that all too clear.

Ecclesiastes 3:19-20 New American Standard Bible (NASB)

¹⁹ For the fate of the sons of men **[humans or people]** and the fate of beasts is the same. As one dies so dies the other; indeed, they all have the same breath and there is no advantage for man over beast, for all is vanity. ²⁰ All go to the same place. All came from the dust and all return to the dust.

In other words, when we breathe our last breath, our cells begin to die. Death is the ending of all vital functions or processes in an organism or cell. When our heart stops beating, our blood is no longer circulating, carrying nourishment and oxygen (by breathing) to the trillions of cells in our body; we are what are termed, clinically dead. However, somatic death has yet to occur, meaning we can be revived, after many minutes of being clinically dead, if the heart and lungs can be restarted again, which gives the cells the oxygen they need.

After about three minutes of clinical death, the brain cells begin to die, meaning the chances of reviving the person is less likely as each second passes. We know that it is vital that the breathing and blood flow be maintained for the life force (*ruach chaiyim*) in the cells. Nevertheless, it is not the lack of breathing or the failure of the heart beating alone, but rather the active life force **("spirit") [Hebrew, ruach]** within the trillions of human cells which make up the human body **+**

breath of life [Hebrew, *neshamah*] that sustains the life force from God.

Psalm 104:29 (ESV)	Psalm 146:4 (ESV)	Ecclesiastes 8:8 (ESV)
29 When you hide your face, they are dismayed; when you take away their breath, they die and return to their dust.	4 When his breath departs, he returns to the earth; on that very day his plans perish.	8 No man has power to retain the spirit, or power over the day of death. There is no discharge from war, nor will wickedness deliver those who are given to it.

Again, …

Ezekiel 18:4 (ESV)	Leviticus 21:1 (ASV)	Numbers 6:6 (ASV)
4 Behold, all souls are mine; the soul of the father as well as the soul of the son is mine: the soul who sins shall die.	21 And Jehovah said to Moses, Speak to the priests, the sons of Aaron, and say to them, There shall none defile himself for the dead **[Or "for a soul."]** among his people;	6 All the days that he separates himself unto Jehovah he shall not come near to a dead body **[Or "soul."]**.

Again, the death of a "soul" means the death of a person ...

1 Kings 19:4 (ASV)	Jonah 4:8 (ASV)	Mark 3:4 (ASV)
4 But he himself went a day's journey into the wilderness, and came and sat down under a juniper-tree: and he requested for himself that he **[Or "his soul.]** "might die, and said, It is enough; now, O Jehovah, take away my life [soul]; for I am not better than my fathers.	8 And it came to pass, when the sun arose, that God prepared a sultry east wind; and the sun beat upon the head of Jonah, that he fainted, and requested for himself that he might die **[Or "that his soul might die."]**, and said, It is better for me to die than to live.	4 And he said to them, Is it lawful on the sabbath day to do good, or to do harm? to save a life **[Or "soul."]**, or to kill? But they held their peace.

As you can see from the above texts, a "soul," or person can die, and the difference between clinical death and somatic death.

What Causes Human Death?

Genesis 2:16-17 Updated American Standard Version (ASV)

[16] And Jehovah God commanded the man, saying, "From every tree of the garden you may freely eat, [17] but from the tree of the knowledge of good and evil you shall not eat,[18] for in the day that you eat from it you shall surely die."[19]

Here we have the first mention of dying within Scripture. It would seem that the death of animals was already the case, as they were not designed to live forever. Thus, when God mentioned the sentence of death for disobeying, Adam knew full well what death was, as he likely had seen many animals die. When Adam disobeyed, he actually rebelled against the sovereignty of God, and this resulted in his death (Gen. 3:19; Jam. 1:14-15) From the moment that Adam ate, his sinful rebellion and its consequences, i.e., death, spread to all of his descendants.

Romans 5:12 (UASV)	**Romans 6:23** (UASV)
[12] Therefore, just as through one man sin entered into the world, and death through sin,	[23] For the wages of sin is death, but the free gift[21] of God is eternal life in Christ Jesus our Lord.

---

[18] Lit *eat from it*

[19] Lit., *dying you* [singular] *shall die.* Heb., *moth tamuth*; the first reference to death in the Scriptures

and so death spread to all men,[20] because all sinned—.	

Some texts are often used to support the idea that physical death was all a part of God's plan; it was an eventuality for humans. One example would be Psalm 90:10, saying, "As for the days of our life, they contain seventy years, or if due to strength, eighty years" Another would be Hebrews 9:27, where Paul says, "inasmuch as it is appointed (Lit laid up) for men to die once and after this *comes* judgment ..."

Was physical death all a part of God's plan for Adam and Eve, since Hebrews 9:27 says, "inasmuch as it is appointed for men to die once and after this comes judgment"?

No, Hebrews 9:27 is not a reference to Adam and Eve, who were created by God so,

(1) that Adam would procreate with Eve and fill the earth with perfect humans that would live forever,

(2) that perfect Adam and Eve and their descendants would cultivate the Garden of Eden until we would have had a

---

[21] Lit., "gracious gift." Gr., *kharisma*

[20] The Greek word *anthropoi* refers here to both men and women; also twice in verse 18

paradise earth, and

(3) that perfect humanity would care for the animals.

Are we to believe that Satan could actually thwart God's intended purpose? Hardly! If Adam and Eve had chosen to obey God, which was possible with their free will, they were looking at being able to live as perfect humans forever. (Genesis 2:15-17) The context of Hebrews 9:27 is applicable to ancient Israel's high priest. On Atonement Day, the high priest foreshadowed Jesus Christ.—Hebrews 4:14-15.

Hebrews chapters 8 and 9 give the reader many details of the Mosaic Law that "serve as a copy and shadow of the heavenly things." (Heb. 8:5) This is especially true of the sacrificial process on the yearly Day of Atonement. It was on this one day each year that the high priest was allowed to enter into the Holy of Holies of the tabernacle. The Holy of Holies was the innermost sanctuary of the temple, which was "separated from the other parts of the temple by a thick curtain, the holy of holies was specially associated with the presence of Yahweh." (*Holman Illustrated Bible Dictionary*, 774) Before the high priest could enter, he had to prepare special incense. The *Holman Illustrated Bible Dictionary* states (387),

"The ceremony began with the sacrifice of a young bull as a sin offering for the priest and his family (Lev. 16:3, 6). After burning incense before the mercy seat in the inner sanctuary, the high priest sprinkled the blood from the bull on and in front of the mercy seat (16:14). The priest cast lots over two goats. One was offered as a sin offering. The other was presented alive as a scapegoat (16:5, 7–10, 20–22). The blood of the goat used as the sin offering was sprinkled like that of the bull to make atonement for the sanctuary (16:15). The mixed blood of the bull and goat were applied to the horns of the altar to make atonement for it (16:18). The high priest confessed all of the people's sins over the head of the live goat which was led away and then released in the wilderness (16:21–22). Following the ceremony, the priest again bathed and put on his usual garments (16:23–24). The priest then offered a burnt offering for the priest and the people (16:24)."

This offering, even if followed to the letter of the Law only lasted until the following year, as it had to be repeated year after year. Continuing his point, Paul said "Christ appeared as a high priest," but after his death and resurrection, "Christ has entered, not into holy places made with hands, which are copies of the true things, but into heaven itself, now to appear in the presence of God on our behalf." (Hebrews 9:11, 12, 24) Yes, Jesus' sacrifice did not need to be repeated, as "he has appeared once for all at the end of the ages to put away sin by the sacrifice of himself." (Heb. 9:25-26; Rom. 6:9) Paul then said,

Hebrews 9:27-28 New American Standard Bible (NASB)

27 And inasmuch as it is appointed for men to die once and after this *comes* judgment,28 so Christ also, having been offered once to bear the sins of many, will appear a second time for salvation without *reference to* sin, to those who eagerly await Him.

After looking at the context, we can now better understand Hebrews 9:27. What most do not comment on when speaking of the priest going into the Holy of Holies each year to offer the atoning sacrifice, he was actually risking his life. If he had fallen short in any way, he would have never made it into the Holy of Holies, as he would have died before being allowed through the curtain. If he had not followed the process as laid out, or he had failed to walk with God aright throughout that previous year, neither he nor his sacrifices would have been accepted as atonement for the people. Therefore, if he fell short it would have meant a condemnation death for him and a condemnation for all he was offering sacrifices for, as they would have not been reconciled to God. Thus, the *judgment* mention in verse 27 was referring to the Day of Atonement and the typical priests.

It is clear that Jesus could have fallen short; otherwise, (1) Satan would have not bothered to tempt him, (2) and the Father would have never sent angels to strengthen him. Therefore, if Jesus had fallen short in any way, he would have not been resurrected on the third day, to go through the curtain into the Holy of Holies, heaven itself. He would have received the *judgment*. Nevertheless, because he was resurrected on the third day, we know that his life, ministry and sacrifice were perfect. When we look at the context of Hebrews 9:27, Paul makes the point that Jesus' sacrifice was superior to the priests that came before him.

We can also look at Hebrews 9:27 in an experiential way for humanity, in that, while Adam and Eve could have lived for an eternity, this has not proved the case for their descendants, as we have not had that opportunity as of yet.

As the reader knows, Adam and Even gave birth to their first child after sinning and being expelled from the Garden of Eden. Thus, "sin came into the world through one man, and death through sin, and so death spread to all men," and "the wages of sin is death." (Rom. 5:12; 6:23) The receiving of the death penalty by way of our ancestor Adam can only be given to us once. If one receives a resurrection, and uses his free will to sin or rebel at a future time, say during the millennium, death will then be the result of his own actions, not the sins of Adam.—Revelation 20:13-15.

On the other hand, those who receive a resurrection and remain faithful, they will receive a favorable judgment of eternal life.—Revelation 21:3-6.

> In Summary, Hebrews 9:27 contextually refer to Jesus as the high priest, in contrast to the former priestly services, in ancient Israel. In addition, it also conveys the general experience of humanity that has received death by way of Adam's sin. Nevertheless, is **unbiblical** to use it as a means of predestination, saying Adam and Eve's physical death was all a part of God's plan.

Yes, these texts were written after the fall of man, after "sin came into the world through one man, and death through sin, and so death spread to all men. (Rom 5:12) We look at those who lived before the flood such as Methuselah, the father of Lamech and grandfather of Noah; he lived 969 years, the longest of Bible record. (Gen. 5:27) This is evidence that God's original intentions were for humans to live forever here on earth.

Humans are alienated from God and are in "slavery to corruption." (Rom. 8:21) This is because sin, missing the mark of perfection is at work within them, resulting in "the works of the flesh." (Gal 5:19-21) Paul tells us, "Let not sin therefore reign in your mortal body, to make you obey its passions." Then he asks, "Do you not know that if you present yourselves to anyone as obedient slaves, you are slaves of the one whom you obey, either of sin, which leads to death, or of obedience, which leads to righteousness?" (Rom. 6:12, 16, See 19-21) Satan "has the power of death" (Heb. 2:14-15) John called him a "murderer from the beginning." (John 8:44) This is not to say that Satan has the capacity to kill humans at will, but because he does so through deception and luring of humans into sin, by prompting or motivating wrongdoing that leads to corruption and death (2 Cor. 11:3), and also by engendering murderous thinking in the minds and hearts of humans. (John 8:40-44, 59; 13:2; See also James 3:14-16; 4:1, 2) Death is the "enemy" of humanity, and not what God had intended for us. (1 Cor. 15:26) The only ones who have ever desired death, even in imperfect bodies and an imperfect world, are those that have suffered immense pain.— Job 3:21, 22; 7:15; Rev. 9:6.

What is the Condition of the Dead?

When the Bible talks about the condition of the dead it presents it in five senses, (1) knowing nothing, (2) asleep like state, (3) powerless, (4) returning to the dust of the ground, (5) and awaiting a resurrection.

First Sense

Ecclesiastes 9:5, 10 English Standard Version (ESV)

⁵ For the living know that they will die, but the dead know nothing, and they have no more reward, for the memory of them is forgotten. ¹⁰ Whatever your hand finds to do, do it with your might, for there is no work or thought or knowledge or wisdom in Sheol [gravedom], to which you are going.

Second Sense

John 11:11 (ESV)	1 Kings 2:10 (ESV)
¹¹ After saying these things, he said to them, "Our friend Lazarus has fallen asleep, but I go to awaken him."	¹⁰ Then David slept with his fathers and was buried in the city of David.

Third Sense

Proverbs 2:18 (ESV)	Isaiah 26:14 (ESV)

¹⁸ for her house sinks down to death,
   and her paths to the departed;
	¹⁴ They are dead, they will not live;
	   they are shades, they will not arise;
	to that end you have visited them with destruction
	   and wiped out all remembrance of them.

Fourth Sense

Genesis 3:19 (ESV)	Ecclesiastes 3:19-20 (NASB)
¹⁹ By the sweat of your face you shall eat bread, till you return to the ground,	¹⁹ For the fate of the sons of men and the fate of beasts is the same. As one dies so dies the

for out of it you were taken; for you are dust, and to dust you shall return."	other; indeed, they all have the same breath and there is no advantage for man over beast, for all is vanity.[20] All go to the same place. All came from the dust and all return to the dust.

Fifth Sense

John 5:28-29 (ESV)	Acts 24:15 (ESV)
[28] Do not marvel at this, for an hour is coming when all who are in the tombs will hear his voice [29] and come out, those who have done good to the resurrection of life, and those who have done evil to the resurrection of judgment.	[15] having a hope in God, which these men themselves accept, that there will be a resurrection of both the just and the unjust.

In death, Scripture shows us as being unable to praise God. The Psalmist tells us, "For in death there is no remembrance of you; in Sheol [gravedom] who will give you praise?" (Psa. 6:5) Isaiah the prophet writes, "For Sheol [gravedom] cannot thank you [God], death cannot praise you; those who go down to the pit cannot hope for your faithfulness. 'It is the living who give thanks to you, as I do today; a father tells his sons about your faithfulness.'" – Isaiah 38:18-19.

Passing Over from Death to Life

John 5:24 English Standard Version (ESV)

24 Truly, truly, I say to you, whoever hears my word and believes him who sent me has eternal life. He does not come into judgment, but has passed from death to life.

Regeneration is God restoring and renewing somebody morally or spiritually, where the Christian receives a new quality of life. This one goes from the road of death over to the path of life. (John 5:24) Here he becomes a new person, with a new personality, having removed the old person. (Eph. 4:20-24) **This does not mean** that the imperfection is gone, and the sinful desires are removed, but that he now has the mind of Christ, the Spirit and the Word of God to gain control over his thinking and his fleshly desires. Therefore, if one has truly experienced a conversion, it will be evident by the changes in one's new personality from the old personality, his life, and his actions. If this is the case, he will be fulfilling the words of Jesus, "let your light shine before others, so that they may see your good works and give glory to your Father who is in heaven." (Matt. 5:16)

Can we see one as truly a man of faith, a committed Christian, who attends the meetings, but he never carries out any personal study, never shares the gospel with another, never helps his spiritual brothers or sisters (physically, materially, mentally, or spiritually), nor helps his neighbor, or any of the other things one would find in a man of faith? James had something to say about this back in chapter 1:26-27, "If anyone thinks he is religious and does not bridle his tongue but deceives his heart, this person's religion is worthless. A Religion that is pure and undefiled before God, the Father, is this: to visit orphans and widows in their affliction, and to keep oneself unstained from the world." One who does not possess real faith, will not help the poor. He will not separate himself from worldly pursuits. He will favor those that he can benefit from (i.e., the powerful and wealthy), and ignore those that he cannot make gains from (i.e., orphans and widows). Moreover, he will not know the love of God, nor his mercy. – James 2:8-9, 13.

Titus 3:5 Lexham English Bible (LEB)

⁵ he saved us, not by deeds of righteousness that we have done, but because of his mercy, **through the washing of regeneration** and renewal by the Holy Spirit,

The Greek word *polingenesia* means to a renewal or rebirth of a new life in Christ, by the Holy Spirit. Jesus told Nicodemus, "unless someone is born of … Spirit, he is not able to enter into the kingdom of God." (John 3:5). At the moment a person is converted, he is regenerated or renewed, passing over from death to life eternal. Jesus explains this in John 5:24, "the one who hears my word and who believes the one who sent me has eternal life, and does not come into judgment, but has passed from death into life." The principal feature of the rebirth of a new life in Christ, by the Holy Spirit, regeneration, is the passing over from death to life eternal.

At that point, the Spirit dwells within this newly regenerated one. From the time of Adam and Eve, God has desired to dwell with man. God fellowshiped with Adam in the Garden of Eden. After Adam's rebellion, he chose faithful men, to walk with him in their life course, to communicate with them. Enoch, Noah, and Abraham walked with God. In the Hebrew language, the tabernacle is called *mishkan* meaning "dwelling place." In both the tabernacle and the temple, God was represented as dwelling with the people in the Most Holy. He also dwelt with the people through the Son, "And the Word became flesh and dwelt among us, and we have seen his glory, glory as of the only Son from the Father, full of grace and truth." (John 1:14) After Jesus' ascension, God dwelt among the Christians, by way of the Holy Spirit, in the body of each individual Christian, which begins at conversion.

Death Thrown into the Lake of Fire

See APPENDIX B

What is the Second Death

Although the expression "first death" does not occur, the concept is implied in Rev. 20:6, which states that "the second death has no power" over "the one who shares in the first resurrection." Sharing in the first resurrection would be impossible unless they had previously died. (Brand, Draper and Archie 2003, 1457)

We have been studying about the first death, namely Adamic death, that which we have inherited from Adam and Eve. If that was the first death, the second death must be distinct from that death. It is clear from the Scriptures that there is a resurrection hope from the first death, but not from the second death.

Revelation 2:11 English Standard Version (ESV)

¹¹ He who has an ear, let him hear what the Spirit says to the churches. The one who conquers will not be hurt by **the second death**.'

The ones who conqueror are guaranteed of immortal heavenly life, which cannot be affected by death.—1 Corinthians 15:53-54.

Revelation 20:6 English Standard Version (ESV)

⁶ Blessed and holy is the one who shares in the first resurrection! Over such **the second death** has no power, but they will be priests of God and of

Christ, and they will reign with him for a thousand years.

Again, the ones who conqueror that share in "the first resurrection" are guaranteed of immortal heavenly life, which cannot be affected by the second death, which will mean annihilation, destruction without hope of a resurrection for those who experience it.

Revelation 20:13-14 English Standard Version (ESV)

¹³ And the sea gave up the dead who were in it, Death and Hades gave up the dead who were in them, and they were judged, each one of them, according to what they had done. ¹⁴ Then Death and Hades were thrown into the lake of fire. This is the **second death**, the lake of fire.

Notice that death, which is what we inherited from our first parents Adam and Eve, as well as Hades (gravedom), is going to be "thrown into the lake of fire." Is not death and Hades abstract, are they able to be tormented and suffer forever. No. However, the fire does picture their eternal destruction, which will take place once they 'give up the dead who were in them.' Note that Paul clearly said, "The last enemy to be destroyed is death." (1 Corinthians 15:26)

The fire and burning within Scripture are merely representing annihilation or eternal destruction. Therefore, there is no eternal torment in Sheol (gravedom), Hades (equivalent of Sheol) hell (English translation), Gehenna (symbol of destruction), or the lake of fire (symbol of destruction). What about the parable of the sheep (righteous) and the goats (wicked), which has the goats, or the wicked going away into eternal punishment?

Revelation 21:8 English Standard Version (ESV)

8 But as for the cowardly, the faithless, the detestable, as for murderers, the sexually immoral, sorcerers, idolaters, and all liars, their portion will be in the lake that burns with fire and sulfur, which is the **second death**."

John speaks of a "lake that burns with fire and sulfur," where the wicked are thrown. It would seem that if hellfire were truth, this would be the place. However, we are simple told by John, this is "the second death," which will mean annihilation, destruction without hope of a resurrection for those who experience it.

Do not be put off by these concepts, because there is more of a detailed explanation coming on this in Chapter 3 and APPENDIX B.

CHAPTER 3 The Hope of a Resurrection - Where?

All of us have lost a loved one to this force to be reckoned with, and it is only a matter of time before we have to face the greatest enemy humankind has ever known, death! However, we have been given a hope that is as great at the penalty that we are under. We have the hope of life eternal, and if we die, it is the hope of a resurrection. This hope means that we will be reunited with the loved ones that we have lost. Some in the past have had a foretaste of this great hope:

Mark 5:35, 41-42 English Standard Version (ESV)

35 While he was still speaking, there came from the ruler's house some who said, "Your daughter is dead. Why trouble the Teacher any further?" 41 Taking her by the hand he said to her, "Talitha cumi," which means, "Little girl, I say to you, arise." 42 And immediately the girl got up and began walking (for she was twelve years of age), and they were immediately overcome with amazement.

Acts 9:36-41 English Standard Version (ESV)

36 Now there was in Joppa a disciple named Tabitha, which, translated, means Dorcas.22 She was

---

22 The Aramaic name Tabitha and the Greek name Dorcas both mean gazelle

full of good works and acts of charity. **37** In those days she became ill and died, and when they had washed her, they laid her in an upper room. **38** Since Lydda was near Joppa, the disciples, hearing that Peter was there, sent two men to him, urging him, "Please come to us without delay." **39** So Peter rose and went with them. And when he arrived, they took him to the upper room. All the widows stood beside him weeping and showing tunics[23] and other garments that Dorcas made while she was with them. **40** But Peter put them all outside, and knelt down and prayed; and turning to the body he said, "Tabitha, arise." And she opened her eyes, and when she saw Peter she sat up. **41** And he gave her his hand and raised her up. Then calling the saints and widows, he presented her alive.

We have already heard of the charges that Satan has risen against God in chapter six of this book. The resurrection hope allows God to let Satan play out his challenges, to resolve the issues that would have otherwise plagued us for an eternity. It is like when you suffer through a painful medical treatment, to enjoy thereafter with all the complications of the issues you had. It is only by means of the greatest resurrection, namely Jesus Christ that we can have this hope.

---

[23] Greek chiton, a long garment worn under the cloak next to the skin

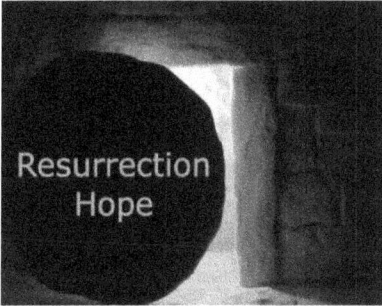

Matthew 20:28 English Standard Version (ESV)

28 even as the Son of Man came not to be served but to serve, and to give his life as a ransom for many.

Resurrection is a Foundational Doctrine

Hebrews 6:1-2 English Standard Version (ESV)

6 Therefore let us leave the elementary doctrine of Christ and go on to maturity, not laying again a foundation of repentance from dead works and of faith toward God, **2** and of instruction about washings,[24] the laying on of hands, the resurrection of the dead and eternal judgment.

The resurrection is a foundational doctrine of our Christian faith. However, it does not fit into the world of humankind that is alienated from God. They see this as the only life there is, and so they are in pursuit of fleshly pleasures, to make the most of it. The mindset of some of the first century was, "If the dead are not raised, 'Let us eat and drink, for tomorrow we die.'" (1 Cor. 15:32, ESV) We, on the other hand, do not need to chase after the things that Satan's world has to offer.

---

[24] Or baptisms (that is, cleansing rites)

Acts 17:32 English Standard Version (ESV)

32 Now when they heard of the resurrection of the dead, some mocked. But others said, "We will hear you again about this."

We need to look to at least two **hopes** that humans have the opportunity of having. Some are of new Israel and is seen as being given a kingdom, a chosen race, a royal priesthood, and ruling with Christ for a thousand years. There will be a need to investigate this, and this section will be a little more complex than any other part of this book. It is very important to all of us, so bear with me. I am going to quote some of the leading evangelical scholars at length.

Revelation 5:9-10 English Standard Version (ESV)

9 And they **sang a new song**, saying,

"Worthy are you to take the scroll
    and to open its seals,
for you were slain, and by your blood you
ransomed people for God
    from every tribe and language and people and
nation,
10 and **you have made them a kingdom and priests** to our God,
    and **they shall reign on**[25] the earth."

_____

[25] According to this verses Jesus will rule "on" the earth. For another consideration, see the next subheading: Over the earth or On the Earth?

A further result of the Lamb's sacrifice is the establishment[26] of the redeemed as a kingdom and priests: *kai epoiēsas autous tǭ theǭ hēmōn basileian kai hiereis* ("and You made them a kingdom and priests to our God"). The threefold occurrence of this theme in Revelation (cf. also Rev. 1:6; 20:6) indicates that talk about such a spiritual heritage was common parlance among Christians of John's day (Swete). As God's possession,[27] the redeemed will not merely be God's people over whom He reigns, but will also share God's rule in the coming millennial kingdom (cf. 1 Cor. 4:8; 6:3) (Charles; Ladd). This kingdom is the goal toward which the program of God is moving as emphasized by *basileusousin* ("they shall reign") later in v. 10 (cf. Rev. 20:4). The idea of priesthood found in *hiereis* ("priests") means full and immediate access into God's presence for the purpose of praise and worship (Ladd). It also includes the thought of priestly service to God (Mounce). Though believers are currently viewed as a royal priesthood (1 Pet. 2:5, 9; cf. Ex. 19:6),

---

[26] The aorist ἐποίησας connotes finished result. As commonly the case in the heavenly songs of this book, it is proleptic, anticipating the culmination of the process being carried out at the time the song is sung (Swete, *Apocalypse*, p. 81; Beckwith, *Apocalypse*, pp. 512–13).[26]

[27] Τῷ θεῷ (5:10) has a possessive sense: "belonging to God" as His peculiar people (Beckwith, *Apocalypse*, p. 513).[27]

this is only preliminary to the fullness of the way they will function alongside Christ in the millennial kingdom.[28]

Kai basileusousin epi tēs gēs ("and they shall reign on the earth") explains more fully the earlier *basileian* ("kingdom"). The fact that believers will serve as reigning powers means that they will be the equivalent of kings (Charles; Beckwith). Spelled out more particularly in 20:4 regarding the millennial kingdom and in 22:5 regarding the eternal state, they will join with Christ in His continual reign following His second advent to the earth. This all stems from the epoch determining redemptive work of the Lamb.[29]

On the earth or Over the Earth

ἐπί **epí** [2093] is in the genitive and can range from: on, upon; over; at, by; before, in the presence of; when, under, at the time of;[30] Below you are going to find a list the genitive epi within Revelation that has a similar construction. Please pay special attention to **5:10, 9:11,** and **11:6**, but there will be others that are similar.

---

[28] Newell, Revelation, p. 13.

[29] Robert L. Thomas, Revelation 1-7: An Exegetical Commentary (Chicago: Moody Publishers, 1992), 402.

[30] William D. Mounce, Mounce's Complete Expository Dictionary of Old & New Testament Words (Grand Rapids, MI: Zondervan, 2006), 1150.

If we are to establish that some translations are choosing a rendering because it suits their doctrine, we must compare how they render the same thing elsewhere. You do not need to be a Greek scholar below, so you can ignore the grammar talk, and just notice the similarities and differences.

I do believe that the English is a problem in trying to say, "they shall reign on the earth." First, because this is not a location issue: i.e., where. The genitive *epi* is dealing not with where, but with authority over, which is expressed by having it over _____ not on _____

Please also take special note that the context of all of these epi genitives that follow the active indicative verb and then are followed by the genitive definite article and noun are dealing with authority.

The verb "to reign" is properly used of kings and queens, and here implies complete power over the world and its inhabitants. So another way of expressing this is "and they shall rule over the world and its inhabitants" or "they shall have power over ...."[31]

---

[31] Bratcher, Robert G.; Hatton, Howard: A Handbook on the Revelation to John. New York: United Bible Societies, 1993 (UBS Handbook Series; Helps for Translators), S. 105

Rev 5:10: basileusousin epi tēs gēs ("They are reigning [opon, on, over] the earth")[32]

ESV: they shall reign **on** the earth

NASB: they will reign **upon** the earth

ASV: they reign **upon** earth

DBY: they shall reign **over** the earth

ἐπί **epí** is in the genitive and comes after the future active indicative verb followed by the definite article and followed by a definite genitive article and noun

Rev 9:11: echousin ep autōn basilea (They are having [upon, on, over] them king)

ESV: They have as king **over** them

NASB: They have as king **over** them

ASV: They have **over** them as king

DBT: They have a king **over** them

ἐπί **epí** is in the genitive and comes after the present active indicative verb followed by a definite genitive article and noun

Rev 11:6: exousian echousin epi tōn hudatōn (they are having authority [upon, on, over] the water)

---

[32] English Standard Version (ESV), New American Standard Bible (NASB), American Standard Version (ASV), and the Darby Bible (DBY)

ESV: they have power **over** the waters

NASB: they have power **over** the waters

ASV: they have power **over** the waters

DBY: they have power **over** the waters

ἐπί **epí** is in the genitive and comes after the future active indicative verb followed by a definite genitive article and noun

Rev 2:26: dōsō autō exousian epi tōn ethnōn (I shall give to him authority [upon, on, over] the nations)

ESV: I will give authority **over** the nations

NASB: I WILL GIVE AUTHORITY **OVER** THE NATIONS

ASV: I give authority **over** the nations

DBY: will I give authority **over** the nations,

ἐπί **epí** is in the genitive and comes after the future active indicative verb followed by a definite genitive article and noun

Rev 6:8: edothē autois exousia epi to tetarton tēs gēs (was given to them authority [upon, on, over] the fourth of the earth)

ESV: they were given authority **over** a fourth of the earth

NASB: Authority was given to them **over** a fourth of the earth

ASV: here was given unto them authority **over** the fourth part of the earth

DBY: authority was given to him **over** the fourth of the earth

ἐπί epí is in the genitive and comes after the future active indicative verb followed by a definite genitive article and noun

Rev 13:7: edothē autō exousia epi pasan phulēn kai laon kai glōssan kai ethnos (was given to it authority [upon, on, over] every tribe and people and tongue and nation)

ESV: authority was given it **over** every tribe and people and language and nation

NASB: authority **over** every tribe and people and tongue and nation was given to him

ASV: there was given to him authority **over** every tribe and people and tongue and nation

DBY: was given to it authority **over** every tribe, and people, and tongue, and nation

ἐπί epí is in the genitive and comes after the future active indicative verb followed by a genitive noun. While there is no definite article, it still seems definite in that we know which one: everyone.

Rev 14:18: ho echōn exousian epi tou puros the one having authority [upon, on, over] the fire

ESV: who has authority **over** the fire

NASB: the one who has power **over** fire

ASV: he that hath power **over** fire

DBY: having power **over** fire

Rev 16:9: tou echontos tēn exousian epi pas plēgas (the one having the authority (upon, on, over) the plagues)

ESV: who had power **over** these plagues

NASB: who has the power **over** these plagues

ASV: who hath the power **over** these plagues

DBY: who had authority **over** these plagues

Rev 17:18: hē polis megalē hē echousa basileian epi tōn basileōn tēs gēs (the woman whom you saw is the city the great the one having kingdom (upon, on, over) the kingdoms of the earth)

ESV: the great city that has dominion **over** the kings of the earth

NASB: the great city, which reigns **over** the kings of the earth.

ASV: the great city, which reigneth **over** the kings of the earth.

DBY: the great city, which has kingship **over** the kings of the earth

Revelation 5:9-10 has a high level of theological content. It either says that Jesus and his co-rulers are going to rule from heaven, over the earth or on the earth. It is theological bias to have several cases of similar context and the same grammatical construction, rendering the verses the same every time, yet to then render one verse contrary to the others, simply because it aligns with one's theology. Whether that is the case here or not, the readers will have to determine for themselves. The point regardless is this, either way, Jesus is ruling the earth, and we are blessed to have had his ransom sacrifice and resurrection. Slow down for the next few pages, as things are going to get a little deeper. We can grasp it if we just slow down meditate on what is being said, and get out our dictionary if we have to, and write the definitions in the book beside the word, and read again.

Heavenly Hope

Revelation 14:1-4 English Standard Version (ESV)

[1] Then I looked, and behold, on Mount Zion stood the Lamb, and with him **144,000** who had his name and his Father's name written on their foreheads. [2] And I heard a voice from heaven like the roar of many waters and like the sound of loud thunder. The voice I heard was like the sound of harpists playing on their harps, [3] and **they were singing a <u>new song</u>** before the throne and before the four living creatures and before the elders. <u>**No one could learn that song except**</u> **the 144,000 who had been redeemed from the earth**. [4] It is these who have not defiled themselves with women, for they are virgins. It is these who

follow the Lamb wherever he goes. These have been redeemed from mankind as firstfruits for God and the Lamb

The whole of chapter 14 is proleptic. As a summary of the Millennium (20:4–6), the first five verses feature the Lamb in place of the beast, the Lamb's followers with His and the Father's seal in place of the beast's followers with the mark of the beast, and the divinely controlled Mount Zion in place of the pagan-controlled earth (Alford, Moffatt, Kiddle).[33]

Revelation 7:4 English Standard Version (ESV)

[4] And I heard the number of the sealed, 144,000, sealed from every tribe of the sons of Israel

Various efforts have sought to determine the significance of the number 144,000. An understanding of the number as symbolical divides it into three of its multiplicands, 12 × 12 × 1000. From the symbolism of the three it is concluded that the number indicates fixedness and fullest completeness.[34] Twelve, a number of the tribes, is both squared and multiplied by a thousand. This is a twofold way of emphasizing completeness (Mounce). It thus affirms the full number of God's people

---

[33] Robert L. Thomas, Revelation 8-22: An Exegetical Commentary (Chicago: Moody Publishers, 1995), 189.

[34] Alford, Greek Testament, 4:624; Charles, Revelation, 1:206; Lenski, Revelation, p. 154.

to be brought through tribulation (Ladd). The symbolic approach points out the impossibility of taking the number literally. It is simply a vast number, less than a number indefinitely great (cf. 7:9), but greater than a large number designedly finite (e.g., 1,000, Rev. 20:2) (Lee). Other occurrences of the numerical components that are supposedly symbolic are also pointed out, 12 thousand in Rev. 21:16, 12 in Rev. 22:2, and 24, a multiple of 12, in Rev. 4:4. This is done to enhance the case for symbolism (Johnson). Though admittedly ingenious, the case for symbolism is exegetically weak. The principal reason for the view is a predisposition to make the 144,000 into a group representative of the church with which no possible numerical connection exists. No justification can be found for understanding the simple statement of fact in v. 4 as a figure of speech. It is a definite number in contrast with the indefinite number of 7:9. If it is taken symbolically, no number in the book can be taken literally. As God reserved 7,000 in the days of Ahab (1 Kings 19:18; Rom. 11:4), He will reserve 144,000 for Himself during the future Great Tribulation.[35] (Thomas,

---

[35] Bullinger, Apocalypse, p. 282. Geyser is correct in observing that the predominant concern of the Apocalypse is "the restoration [on earth] of the twelve tribes of Israel, their restoration as a twelve-tribe kingdom, in a renewed and purified city of David, under

Revelation 1-7: An Exegetical Commentary 1992, 473-74)

These ones are made up of those under the new covenant, the Law of Christ, those **called out of natural Israel**, the new Israelites, also known as the Israel of God. They are a chosen number that are to reign with Jesus as kings, priests, and judges. Therefore, we ask, what is the other hope?

The New Earth: The Earthly Hope

In the O[ld] T[estament] the kingdom of God is usually described in terms of a redeemed earth; this is especially clear in the book of Isaiah, where the final state of the universe is already called new heavens and a new earth (65:17; 66:22) The nature of this renewal was perceived only very dimly by OT authors, but they did express the belief that a humans ultimate destiny is an earthly one.[36]

---

the rule of the victorious 'Lion of the Tribe of Judah, the Root of David' (5:5; 22:16)" (Albert Geyser, "The Twelve Tribes in Revelation: Judean and Judeo Christian Apocalypticism," NTS 23, no. 3 [July 1982]: 389). He is wrong, however, in his theory that this belief characterized the Judean church only and was not shared by Gentile Christianity spearheaded by Paul (ibid., p. 390).

[36] It is unwise to speak of the written Word of God as if it were of human origin, saying 'OT authors express the belief,' when what was written is the meaning and

This vision is clarified in the N[ew] T[estament]. Jesus speaks of the "renewal" of the world (Matt 19:28), Peter of the restoration of all things (Acts 3:21). Paul writes that the universe will be redeemed by God from its current state of bondage (Rom. 8:18-21). This is confirmed by Peter, who describes the new heavens and the new earth as the Christian's hope (2 Pet. 3:13). Finally, the book of Revelation includes a glorious vision of the end of the present universe and the creation of a new universe, full of righteousness and the presence of God. The vision is confirmed by God in the awesome declaration: "I am making everything new!" (Rev. 21:1-8)

The new heavens and the new earth will be the renewed creation that will fulfill the purpose for which God created the universe. It will be characterized by the complete rule of God and by the full realization of the final goal of redemption: "Now the dwelling of God is with men" (Rev. 21:3).

The fact that the universe will be created anew[37] shows that God's goals for humans is not an ethereal and disembodied existence,

---

message of what God wanted to convey by means of the human author.

[37] Create anew does not mean a complete destruction followed by a re-creation, but instead a renewal of the present universe.

but a bodily existence on a perfected earth. The scene of the beatific vision is the new earth. The spiritual does not exclude the created order and will be fully realized only within a perfected creation. (Elwell 2001, 828-29)

What have we learned so far in this publication? God created the earth to be inhabited, to be filled with perfect humans, who are over the animals, and under the sovereignty of God. (Gen 1:28; 2:8, 15; Ps 104:5; 115:16; Eccl 1:4) Sin did not dissuade God from his plans (Isa. 45:18); hence, he has saved redeemable humankind by Jesus ransom sacrifice. It seems that the Bible offers two hopes to redeemed humans, **(1) a heavenly hope**, or **(2) an earthly hope**. It also seems that those with the heavenly hope are limited in number, and are going to heaven to rule with Christ as kings, priests, and judges either **on** the earth or **over** the earth from heaven. It seems that those with the earthly hope are going to receive everlasting life here on a paradise earth as originally intended.

APPENDIX A Genesis 5:24 Did Enoch Go to Heaven?

Hebrews 11:5 English Standard Version (ESV)

5 By faith, Enoch was taken away so that he did not experience death, and he was not to be found because God took him away. For before his transformation he was approved, having pleased God.

Some translators have chosen to go beyond the Scripture, being more in the realms of an interpretative translation. The Message Bible reads, "By an act of faith, Enoch skipped death completely." Worse still the James Moffatt translation states, "It was by faith that Enoch was taken to heaven so that he never died." All the original says is that "Enoch was taken away;" (why), "so that he did not experience death." We need to work within what was written and no subject the text to our preconceived doctrinal ideas. Let us look at what Jesus adds to this . . .

John 3:13 Holman Christian Standard Bible (HCSB)

13 No one has ascended into heaven except the One who descended from heaven, the Son of Man.

This is stated by the Son of God, who existed in heaven at the very time "Enoch was taken away so that he did not experience death." We know two primary points from Jesus' exchange with Nicodemus: (1) Jesus had been in heaven before coming to the earth, and (2) no one was ever to ascend to heaven but those who were 'born again.' It is only by faith in Jesus ransom sacrifice that ones can be born again.

Since only Jesus himself had been in heaven before coming to earth, he speaks with authority. Tenney offers a great line here: "Revelation, not discovery, is the basis for faith" (Tenney, EBC, p. 48). Some Jews of Nicodemus's day taught that great saints would attain heaven by their godliness and righteous living. But no one ever sees heaven apart from the new birth.[38]

Digging Deeper

Here again, digging deeper we look to another New Testament writer, the Apostle Paul, who wrote . . .

Hebrews 11:13, 39 Holman Christian Standard Bible (HCSB)

[13] These all died in faith without having received the promises, but they saw them from a distance, greeted them, and confessed that they were foreigners and temporary residents on the earth. [39] All these were approved through their faith, but they did not receive what was promised,

All prior true followers of God before Jesus' ransom sacrifice would "died in faith."

---

[38] Kenneth O. Gangel, vol. 4, John, Holman New Testament Commentary; Holman Reference (Nashville, TN: Broadman & Holman Publishers, 2000), 53.

The promises for which believers eagerly waited appeared only in Christ. Old Testament saints did not experience the eternal inheritance. Their faith earned for them a remarkable reputation and favor with God. They lived and died in the hope of a fulfillment that none of them saw on earth. The reaping of the benefits did not occur until Christ opened the box of spiritual treasures.[39]

Why would these ones not receive a heavenly inheritance at death, before Jesus' ransom sacrifice? All of humankind has inherited sin from Adam, including Enoch. (Psalm 51:5; Romans 5:12) As man would come to find out in the era of the New Testament, the only means of salvation is by means of Jesus' ransom sacrifice. (Acts 4:12; 1 John 2:1, 2) Enoch lived three thousand years before Jesus' days on the earth, and that ransom had not been paid at that time. Therefore, Enoch was simply asleep in death, awaiting a future resurrection. John 5:28-29

How then are we understand the phrase, "he did not experience death"? Enoch was an outstanding example of faith. "Enoch walked with God, and he was not there because God took him." (Gen 5:18, 21-24; Heb 11:5; 12:1) He was a prophet of God, prophesying of God's coming "with thousands of His holy ones to execute judgment on all, and to convict them of all their ungodly deeds

---

[39] Thomas D. Lea, vol. 10, Hebrews, James, Holman New Testament Commentary; Holman Reference (Nashville, TN: Broadman & Holman Publishers, 1999), 206.

that they have done in an ungodly way, and of all the harsh things ungodly sinners have said against Him." Jude 14-15.

Enoch only lived 365 years in an era where everyone lived over 900 years because God "God took him." Why would God take the only man walking with Him at the time? There is no doubt that this evil world was about to persecute Enoch for his prophecies, to the point of executing him. Instead of letting Satan and the wicked men of that day torture and kill this one faithful follower, God chose to take him in such a way, so as to not experience death. While we do not know how God did this, it is possible that he could have given Enoch a vision, and while, in that vision, Jehovah took him so that he would not experience the pains of death. God had chosen to do a similar thing with Moses as well, disposing of his body. (Deut. 34:5-6; Jude 9) Like some other Bible details, we cannot be dogmatic. However, we can be certain of the following: (1) God took Enoch, (2) so he would not experience death, (3) but he did enter the sleep of death in such a way as to not experience that entry, (4) and had the hope of a future resurrection, (5) based on Jesus' ransom sacrifice.

APPENDIX B Hellfire - Eternal Torment?

Hundreds of millions of both Catholic and Protest Christians have long held that hell is a place of eternal torment for the damned. According to the Encarta Encyclopedia, "Hell, in theology, any place or state of punishment and privation for human souls after death. More strictly, the term is applied to the place or state of eternal punishment of the damned, whether angels or human beings. The doctrine of the existence of hell is derived from the principle of the necessity for the vindication of divine justice, combined with the human experience that evildoers do not always appear to be punished adequately in their lifetime. Belief in a hell was widespread in antiquity and is found in most religions of the world today."

However, it would seem that hellfire and brimstone have lost their spark. The same encyclopedia goes on to say, "In modern times the belief in physical punishment after death and the endless duration of this punishment has been rejected by many. The question about the nature of the punishment of hell is equally controversial. Opinions range from holding the pains of hell to be no more than the remorse of conscience to the traditional belief that the "pain of loss" (the consciousness of having forfeited the vision of God and the happiness of heaven) is combined with the "pain of sense" (actual physical torment).[40]

Probably the most famous hellfire and brimstone preacher was Jonathan Edwards (1703-1758), used to put the fear of God into the hearts and minds of the 18th-century Colonial Americans with detail, explicit, lifelike, word pictures of hell

"Sinners in the Hands of an Angry God" Known for his fiery sermons, clergyman Jonathan Edwards helped start the Great Awakening, an American religious revival of the 1740s.

The God that holds you over the pit of hell, much as one holds a spider, or some loathsome insect over the fire, abhors you, and is dreadfully provoked: his wrath towards you burns like fire; he looks upon you as worthy of nothing else, but to be cast into the fire; he is of purer eyes than to bear to have you in his sight; you are ten thousand times more abominable in his eyes, than the most hateful venomous serpent is in ours. You have offended him infinitely more than ever a stubborn rebel did his prince; and yet it is nothing but his hand that holds you from falling into the fire every moment.

O sinner! Consider the fearful danger you are in: it is a great furnace of wrath, a

---

[40] Microsoft ® Encarta ® 2006. © 1993-2005 Microsoft Corporation. All rights reserved.

wide and bottomless pit, full of the fire of wrath, that you are held over in the hand of that God, whose wrath is provoked and incensed as much against you, as against many of the damned in hell. You hang by a slender thread, with the flames of divine wrath flashing about it, and ready every moment to singe it, and burn it asunder;[41]

Like Edwards, many other Catholic and Protestant preachers, say that God has this eternal place in the offing for the wicked. However, what does the Bible really teach?

Hell

Without being bogged down in doctrinal issues, let us just deal with the facts. "Hell" is the English translation for the Hebrew word Sheol and the Greek word Hades. Therefore, we need not ask, what Hell is. However, what did the word mean when it was first placed in English translations? Webster's Eleventh New International Dictionary, under "Hell" says: [Middle English, from Old English; akin to Old English helan to conceal, Old High German helan, Latin celare, Greek kalyptein]

---

[41] Edwards, Jonathan (2010-05-20). Sinners In The Hands Of An Angry God (Kindle Locations 151-152). Old Land Mark Publishing. Kindle Edition.

before 12th century"[42] The word "hell" meant to 'cover' over or 'conceal,' so it would have meant a place 'covered' or 'concealed,' such as a grave.

Sheol

Webster's Dictionary, "[Hebrew Shĕ'ōl] 1597: the abode of the dead in early Hebrew thought"[43] Collier's Encyclopedia (1986, Vol. 12, p. 28) says: "Since Sheol in Old Testament times referred simply to the abode of the dead and suggested no moral distinctions, the word 'hell,' as understood today, is not a happy translation." Some translations choose to use a transliteration, Sheol, as opposed to the English hell, AT, RSV, ESV, LEB, HCSB, and NASB.

Hades

Everyone knows that Hades was "the underground abode of the dead in Greek mythology."[44] However, as far as early Christianity, the Greek translation of the Old Testament, the

---

[42] Frederick C. Mish, "Preface," *Merriam-Webster's Collegiate Dictionary.* (Springfield, MA: Merriam-Webster, Inc., 2003). hell

[43] Frederick C. Mish, "Preface," *Merriam-Webster's Collegiate Dictionary.* (Springfield, MA: Merriam-Webster, Inc., 2003). sheol

[44] Frederick C. Mish, "Preface," *Merriam-Webster's Collegiate Dictionary.* (Springfield, MA: Merriam-Webster, Inc., 2003). hades

Septuagint, uses the word Hades 73 times, employing it 60 times to translate the Hebrew word Sheol. Luke at Acts 2:27 write, "For you will not abandon my soul to Hades, or let your Holy One see corruption." Luke was quoting Psalm 16:10, which reads, "For you will not abandon my soul to Sheol, or let your holy one see corruption." Notice that Luke used Hades in place of Sheol. Therefore, Hades is the Greek equivalent of Sheol, as far as Christians and the Greek New Testament is concerned. In other words, Hades is also the abode of the dead in early Christian thought. Some translations choose to use a transliteration, Hades, as opposed to the English hell, ASV, AT, RSV, ESV, LEB, HCSB, and NASB.

Gehenna

Gehenna Hebrew Ge' Hinnom, literally, valley of Hinnom appears 12 times in the Greek New Testament books, and many translators render it by the word "hell." Most translations have chosen poorly not to use a transliteration, Gehenna or Geenna, as opposed to the English hell, ASV, AT, RSV, ESV, LEB, HCSB, and NASB. There is little doubt that the New Testament writers and Jesus used "Gehenna" to speak of the place of final punishment. What was Gehenna?

According to the Holman Illustrated Bible Dictionary (p. 632), Gehenna or the Valley of Hinnom was "the valley south of Jerusalem now called the Wadi er-Rababi (Josh. 15:8; 18:16; 2

Chron. 33:6; Jer. 32:35) became the place of child sacrifice to foreign gods. The Jews later used the valley for the dumping of refuse, the dead bodies of animals, and executed criminals."[45] We would disagree with the other comments by the Holman Illustrated Dictionary, "The continuing fires in the valley (to consume the refuse and dead bodies) apparently led the people to transfer the name to the place where the wicked dead suffer." This just is not the case.

In the Old Testament, the Israelites did burn sons in the fires as part of a sacrifice to false gods, but not for the purpose of punishment, or torture. By the time of the New Testament period, hundreds of years later, the only thing thrown in Gehenna was trash and the dead bodies of executed criminals. For what purpose were these thrown into Gehenna? It was used as an incinerator, a furnace for destroying things by burning them. Notice that any bodies thrown in Gehenna during the New Testament period were already dead. Thus, if anything, these people saw Gehenna as a place where they destroyed their trash and the bodies of dead criminals. Thus, if Jesus used this to illustrate the place of the wicked, it would have represented destruction as the punishment.

---

[45] Chad Brand et al., eds., "Gehenna," *Holman Illustrated Bible Dictionary* (Nashville, TN: Holman Bible Publishers, 2003), 632.

How Are We to Understand the "Fire"?

Mark 9:43-48 English Standard Version (ESV)

43 And if your hand causes you to sin, cut it off. It is better for you to enter life crippled than with two hands to go to hell, to the unquenchable fire.**45** And if your foot causes you to sin, cut it off. It is better for you to enter life lame than with two feet to be thrown into hell. **47** And if your eye causes you to sin, tear it out. It is better for you to enter the kingdom of God with one eye than with two eyes to be thrown into hell, **48** 'where their worm does not die and the fire is not quenched.'

Matthew 13:42 English Standard Version (ESV)

42 and throw them into the fiery furnace. In that place there will be weeping and gnashing of teeth.

Here is why we should use the transliteration as opposed to the English "hell." Jesus did not use the word "Hades" in the above texts, the equivalent of Sheol, but rather Gehenna. Jesus used comparisons in his teaching, using things that his listeners could relate. As we learned in the above Gehenna was a garbage dump that was used as an incinerator, to destroy whatever was thrown in, and only the bodies of criminals were thrown in after they were already dead. In other words, the fire was used as a symbol, not of torment, but rather of being destroyed, complete destruction, namely annihilation by fire.

What did Jesus mean by "there will be weeping and gnashing of teeth"? We can look at what he said about those, who believed they were on the right path,

Matthew 7:21-23 English Standard Version (ESV)

21 "Not everyone who says to me, 'Lord, Lord,' will enter the kingdom of heaven, but the one who does the will of my Father who is in heaven. 22 On that day many will say to me, 'Lord, Lord, did we not prophesy in your name, and cast out demons in your name, and do many mighty works in your name?' 23 And then will I declare to them, 'I never knew you; depart from me, you workers of lawlessness.'

In other words, those who will be weeping and gnashing of teeth" are those who believed they had the truth, but did not. Can we imagine giving our whole life to what we think to be the correct path, only to get to the edge and discover, we are on the wrong path because we chose to do our will, not the will of the Father? Now then, what about what John penned in the book of Revelation?

Revelation 21:8 English Standard Version (ESV)

8 But as for the cowardly, the faithless, the detestable, as for murderers, the sexually immoral, sorcerers, idolaters, and all liars, their portion will be in the lake that burns with fire and sulfur, which is the second death."

John speaks of a "lake that burns with fire and sulfur," where the wicked are thrown. It would seem that if hellfire were the truth, this would be the place. However, we are simply told by John; this is "the second death." Moreover, he had told his readers earlier,

Revelation 20:13-14 English Standard Version (ESV)

¹³ And the sea gave up the dead who were in it, Death and Hades gave up the dead who were in them, and they were judged, each one of them, according to what they had done. ¹⁴ Then Death and Hades were thrown into the lake of fire. This is the second death, the lake of fire.

Notice that death, which is what we inherited from our first parents Adam and Eve, as well as Hades (gravedom), is going to be "thrown into the lake of fire." Is not death and Hades abstract, are they able to be tormented and suffer forever. No. However, the fire does picture their eternal destruction, which will take place once they 'give up the dead who were in them.' Note that Paul clearly said, "The last enemy to be destroyed is death." – 1 Corinthians 15:26.

The fire and burning within Scripture are simply representing annihilation or eternal destruction. Therefore, there is no eternal torment in Sheol (gravedom), Hades (the equivalent of Sheol) hell (English translation), Gehenna (symbol of destruction), or the lake of fire (symbol of destruction). What about the parable of the sheep (righteous) and the goats (wicked), which has the goats, or the wicked going away into eternal punishment?

Matthew 25:46 English Standard Version (ESV)

[46] And these will go away into eternal punishment [*Kolasin*], but the righteous into eternal life."

Kolasin "akin to *kolazoo*"[46] "This means 'to cut short,' 'to lop,' 'to trim,' and figuratively a. 'to impede,' 'restrain,' and b. 'to punish,' and in the passive 'to suffer loss.'[47] The first part of the sentence is only in harmony with the second part of the sentence, if the eternal punishment is eternal death. The wicked receive eternal death and the righteous eternal life. We might at that Matthews Gospel was primarily for the Jewish Christians, and under the Mosaic Law, God would punish those who violated the law, saying they "shall be cut off [penalty of death] from Israel." (Ex 12:15; Lev 20:2-3) We need further to consider,

---

[46] W. E. Vine, Merrill F. Unger, and William White Jr., Vine's Complete Expository Dictionary of Old and New Testament Words (Nashville, TN: T. Nelson, 1996), 498.

[47] Gerhard Kittel, Gerhard Friedrich, and Geoffrey William Bromiley, Theological Dictionary of the New Testament (Grand Rapids, MI: W.B. Eerdmans, 1985), 451.

2 Thessalonians 1:8-9 English Standard Version (ESV)

⁸ in flaming fire, inflicting vengeance on those who do not know God and on those who do not obey the gospel of our Lord Jesus. ⁹ They will suffer the punishment of eternal destruction, away from the presence of the Lord and from the glory of his might

Notice that Paul says too that the punishment for the wicked is "eternal destruction." Many times in talking with those that support the position of eternal torment in some hellfire, they will add a word to Matthew 25:46 in their paraphrase of the verse, 'eternal conscious punishment.' However, Jesus does not tell us what the eternal punishment is, just that it is a punishment, and it is eternal. Therefore, those who support eternal conscious fiery torment will read the verse to mean just that, while those, who hold the position of eternal destruction, will take Matthew 25:46 to mean that. Considering that Jesus does not define what the eternal punishment is, this verse is not a proof text for either side of the argument. Does Jesus' parable, The Rich Man, and Lazarus, not support the hellfire doctrine? (Luke 16:19-31)

Interpreting Parables

Jesus gave us some 40 parables or illustrations, filling them with symbols and images that represented a message he was trying to share. Now, we get to this one, and we want to take it literally? Robert H. Stein writes,

> Similarly, the parable of the rich man and Lazarus (Luke 16:19–31) is to be interpreted as a parable, and thus according to the rules governing the interpretation of parables. It is not to be interpreted as a historical account. (Luke reveals this by the introduction "A certain man ..." which is used in the Gospel to introduce parables [cf. Luke 10:30; 14:16; 15:11; 16:1; 19:12]. This is clearer in the Greek text than in most translations, but it is fairly obvious in the NASB.)[48]

In discussing interpretation rules, stein goes on to say,

> In a similar way, there are different "game" rules involved in the interpretation of the different kinds of biblical literature. The author has played his "game," has sought to convey his meaning, under the rules covering the particular literary form he used. Unless we know those rules, we will almost certainly misinterpret his meaning. If we interpret a parable (Luke 16:19–31) as if it were narrative, or if we interpret poetry (Judg. 5) as if it were narrative, we will err. Similarly, if we interpret a narrative such as the resurrection of Jesus

---

[48] Robert H. Stein, A Basic Guide to Interpreting the Bible: Playing by the Rules (Grand Rapids, MI: Baker Books, 1994), 30.

(Matt. 28:1–10) as a parable, we will also err
(1 Cor. 15:12–19).[49]

Step One in Understanding Parables

Read the context of the parable. You need to find out the setting of the parable, looking for the conditions and the circumstances. Why was the parable told? What prompted its being told?

Step Two in Understanding Parables

Consider the cultural backgrounds, such as the laws and customs of the setting, as well as the idioms that were spoken of earlier.

Step Three in Understanding Parables

This is a two-point step. The first point is to look to the author of the parable for the upcoming meaning of the parable. An interpreter of a parable by Jesus would see what he meant in the context it was spoken, and then consider his teaching as a whole. The second point is, do not assign subjective meanings to the elements of a parable. Generally, a parable teaches one basic point.

Stage One: Discovering the Main Characters

In any given parable, it is highly important to find the main 2–3 characters.

---

[49] IBID., 76.

Stage Two: Looking to the End

As is true with any kind of story, the end of the story carries the weight of importance. This is no different with parables. The ending is where the answers lie.

Stage Three: Who Carries the Conversation

Which character carries the conversation?

Stage Four: Who Gets the Most Press

Generally, whoever gets the most coverage in a story is the primary character, followed by the secondary person that must exist to facilitate the story and its main point.[50]

The setting of the parable of The rich man and Lazarus (Lu 16:19-31) is Jesus speaking, with the Pharisees listening in, who were well known as one who hungered for riches. What was Jesus teaching by this parable?

It had nothing to do with punishment for sin. It had to do with two different groups of people, the rich man (Jewish religious leaders) and the beggar Lazarus (poor Jewish people), as there was about to be a drastic change in their privileged and lowly positions. The Rich man, the Jewish religious leaders, opposed Jesus and the Good News of the

---

[50] Edward D. Andrews, A BASIC GUIDE TO BIBLICAL INTERPRETATION Understanding the Correct Methods of Interpretation (Christian Publishing House, Cambridge, OH, 2014), 313.

Kingdom that he brought because he was busy sharing it with the common Jewish people. This, in fact, tormented the Jewish religious leaders to no end, to the point of their seeking to kill him. (Luke 20:19, 20, 46, 47) Conversely, the beggar Lazarus represents, the poor, common Jewish people, who were looked upon with disdain, like beggars by the Jewish religious leaders, were being given the privilege position of becoming disciples of Jesus, and the first to enter into the kingdom.—1 Cor. 1:26-29.

What is the meaning of the "tormented with fire and sulfur" in Revelation 14:9-11?

Revelation 14:9-11 English Standard Version (ESV)

⁹ And another angel, a third, followed them, saying with a loud voice, "If anyone worships the beast and its image and receives a mark on his forehead or on his hand, ¹⁰ he also will drink the wine of God's wrath, poured full strength into the cup of his anger, and he will be tormented with fire and sulfur in the presence of the holy angels and in the presence of the Lamb. ¹¹ And the smoke of their torment goes up forever and ever, and they have no rest, day or night, these worshipers of the beast and its image, and whoever receives the mark of its name."

In the above text, those who worshipping the symbolic "beast and its image," they will be "tormented with fire and sulfur." The context here is not what happens after these one's deaths, but rather what happens to them while they are alive. What is it that torments these ones while they are alive? It is the proclamations of Christians that worshipers of the "beast and its image" will experience, to such a level that it is referred to as "tormented with fire and sulfur." Looking at the context of 14:11, it is not the torment that lasts forever; it is 'the smoke of their torment that goes up forever and ever.' What is smoke is a signal of their symbolic burning that will rise forever because the lesson learned will never be forgotten. Is there yet another example of this in Scripture? Yes.

The Judgment of Edom

Isaiah 34:9-12 English Standard Version (ESV)

⁹ And the streams of Edom shall be turned into pitch,
    and her soil into sulfur;
    her land shall become burning pitch.
¹⁰ Night and day it shall not be quenched;
its smoke shall go up forever.
From generation to generation it shall lie waste;
    none shall pass through it forever and ever.
¹¹ But the hawk and the porcupine shall possess it,
    the owl and the raven shall dwell in it.
He shall stretch the line of confusion over it,
    and the plumb line of emptiness.
¹² Its nobles—there is no one there to call it a kingdom,
    and all its princes shall be nothing.

Was Edom thrown into some literal hellfire to burn forever? No. The Edomite nation, an enemy of God's people, was removed, which is described in the above in poetic terms, highly symbolic language. It was as though fire and sulfur consumed Edom. If we were to go to the geographical location of ancient Edom, would we see smoke still rising? No. The smoke was and still is today, a signal of a lesson learned from the destruction that Edom faced. This smoke filled lesson will rise forever, in that the lesson learned will live on forever through the Word of God. After Jesus destroys the last enemy death, is it believed that the Bible will no longer be needed? The Bible is a book that will stand forever, as a signal of what humanity already experienced. Let us take this one step further as we look at our next text that is often drawn on to support hellfire doctrine.

Revelation 20:10 English Standard Version (ESV)

¹⁰ and the devil who had deceived them was thrown into the lake of fire and sulfur where the beast and the false prophet were, and they will be tormented (Greek, *basanos*) day and night forever and ever.

The Greek word used here for "torment," *basanizo*, primarily means "to test by rubbing on the touchstone" (basanos, "a touchstone"), then, "to question by applying torture."[51] The Bible is our case law (law established by previous verdicts), which will serve as a touchstone[52] (a standard by which something is judged) that humans were never designed to walk on their own, but to live under the sovereignty of their Creator. The issues raised by Satan will have been settled by humanities walking through thousands of years of an object lesson, for which the Bible is the case law, the touchstone, which will be around forever, as a reminder of the issues raised and settled.

The Moral Test

We know that man and woman were created in the image of God, and so when we hear of people who have tortured criminals, we call that inhumane. Would we expect that the One, whose image we are made in would see the eternal torment of sinners as humane? This would be incompatible with the very person of God. How are we to know how God views justice?

---

[51] W. E. Vine, Merrill F. Unger, and William White Jr., Vine's Complete Expository Dictionary of Old and New Testament Words (Nashville, TN: T. Nelson, 1996), 176.

[52] A touchstone is a hard black stone formerly used to test the purity of gold and silver according to the color of the streak left when the metal was rubbed against it.

(Exodus 21:23-24) But if there is harm, then you shall pay life for life, eye for eye, tooth for tooth, hand for hand, foot for foot,

(Leviticus 24:20) fracture for fracture, eye for eye, tooth for tooth; whatever injury he has given a person shall be given to him.

(Deuteronomy 19:21) Your eye shall not pity. It shall be life for life, eye for eye, tooth for tooth, hand for hand, foot for foot.

(Judges 1:7) And Adoni-bezek said, "Seventy kings with their thumbs and their big toes cut off used to pick up scraps under my table. As I have done, so God has repaid me." And they brought him to Jerusalem, and he died there.

(Matthew 5:38-42) "You have heard that it was said, 'An eye for an eye and a tooth for a tooth.' But I say to you, Do not resist the one who is evil. But if anyone slaps you on the right cheek, turn to him the other also. And if anyone would sue you and take your tunic, let him have your cloak as well. And if anyone forces you to go one mile, go with him two miles. Give to the one who begs from you, and do not refuse the one who would borrow from you."

The above texts are but a few of how God views justice, and it is all too clear that he sees it as the punishment needs to be proportionate, to be the best response to crime. In other words, if an Israelite were to steal his neighbor's cow, he would have to replace it with the cow, and any financial

114

loss he suffered, even some extra as punitive damages. However, would God expect that thief to have to work as a slave to his neighbor for the rest of his life, and his children and grand children's lives as well? Note that that punishment would be way out of proportion to the crime.

Now, let us look at the punishment that God gave Adam and Eve if they were to rebel sinfully, rejecting him and his sovereignty, by choosing to eat from the tree he had commanded them not to eat from.

Genesis 2:17 English Standard Version (ESV)

[17] but of the tree of the knowledge of good and evil you shall not eat, for in the day that you eat of it you shall surely die."

Eat from the tree (i.e., reject God as sovereign) = death. The punishment for sin was death. Please go back and look at Genesis 2:17 in the Bible, in several different translations. Do we notice some footnote from God that said, "And 4,000 years from now, when Jesus arrives, I am going to change the sentence from death to eternal torment in some literal lake of fire?"

Imagine we live in some small American town. We get our driver's licenses. Then, one day, we are pulled over for going 35-Miles Per Hour (MPH) in a 25 MPH zone. The police officer writes us a ticket and tells us to appear in court the following month, where the judge will fine us $50.00. We arrive at court the next month, and are in front of the magistrate, and he just found us guilty and sentences us not to a $50.00 fine, but to be taken outside of the courthouse and shot to death by a firing squad. Would anyone suggest that the punishment of a death sentence was proportionate to the crime of a speeding ticket? Would anyone find justice in the law enforcement officer saying the penalty was a mere $50.00 fine, and then the judge later raising the penalty to such an extreme level of capital punishment? God gave Adam the sentence of death, for committing the greatest sin of any human in history, as he had rejected God in perfection, and sentencing billions to death along with him. Would it then be justice, for God to raise the punishment bar to eternal torment in the Lake of Fire? Let us now look at imperfect humanity.

(Romans 3:23) for all have sinned and fall short of the glory of God,

(Romans 5:12) therefore, just as sin came into the world through one man, and death through sin, and so death spread to all men because all sinned

(Romans 6:7) For one who has died has been set free from sin.

(Romans 6:23) For the wages of sin is death, but the free gift of God is eternal life in Christ Jesus our Lord.

If Adam commits the greatest sin a human could commit, and he gets death, how is it justice that imperfect humans are supposedly getting eternal torment in a Lake of Fire?

There are five factors to imperfect humans being even less culpable (Guilty) than Adam was. **(1)** We are imperfect and live in an imperfect world, compounded by the fact that God's Word says we are mentally bent and lean toward doing bad. We read, "When the LORD saw that the wickedness of man on the earth was great and that the whole bent of his thinking was never anything but evil, the LORD regretted that he had ever made man on the earth." (Gen. 6:5, AT) **(2)** We have a wicked spirit creature, Satan the Devil, who is misleading the entire world of humankind. We read, "Be sober-minded; be watchful. Your adversary the devil prowls around like a roaring lion, seeking someone to devour." (1 Pet 5:8, ESV) **(3)** We live in a world that caters to the imperfect flesh. We read, "For all that is in the world, the desires of the flesh and the desires of the eyes and pride in possessions, is not from the Father but is from the world. And the world is passing away along with its desires, but whoever does the will of God abides forever." (1 John 2:16-17) **(4)** We are unable to understand our inner person, which the Bible informs us is wicked: "The heart is deceitful above all things and desperately sick; who can understand it?" (Jer. 17:9) **(5)** In imperfection, man is unable of directing his own step. – Jeremiah 10:23.

Unlike Adam, we are imperfect from the start, and Adam received death for sin. Adam was perfect, with the natural desire to do good, he was mentally perfect, and he lived in a paradise, in direct communication with God. We are born mentally bent toward sin. We have Satan and demons after us. Our natural desire is toward bad. We have an imperfect, fallen world that surrounds us, which caters to our flesh desires. We have a heart (i.e., inner person) that is deceitful and desperately sick and are unable to walk on our own. Thus, who can make the case that it is right, and just that imperfect humans are to receive eternal torment in some literal Lake of Fire? If one who dies, is freed from sin, by having paid the wages of sin, which was paid for through death (Rom 6:23), not the ransom of Christ, why should he then be liable so at to have to suffer eternally in some fiery torment?

If humanity were punishing another human being with deliberate torture of fire, we would find this to be sickening and abhorrent. Our finding it so sickening and abhorrent is actually based on the conscience that God gave man, that same man, who was made in the image of God. This same God clearly stated that such an idea would never have even come into his mind.

Jeremiah 7:31 English Standard Version (ESV)

[31] And they have built the high places of Topheth, which is in the Valley of the Son of Hinnom, to burn their sons and their daughters in the fire, which I did not command, **nor did it come into my mind**.

APPENDIX C Is the Hellfire Doctrine Truly Just?

Genesis 1:27-28 English Standard Version (ESV)

27 So God created man in his own image, in the image of God he created him; male and female he created them.

28 And God blessed them. And God said to them, "Be fruitful and multiply and fill the earth and subdue it, and have dominion over the fish of the sea and over the birds of the heavens and over every living thing that moves on the earth."

It was God's intention that his first couple, namely, Adam and Eve were to procreate, and cultivate the Garden of Eden until it covered the entire earth, filled with humans worshipping him. – Genesis 1:28

If the first couple had not rebelled, they and their offspring could have lived forever.--Genesis 2:15-17

One of the angels in heaven (who became Satan), abused his free will (James 1:14-15). He then willfully chose to rebel against God. Satan used a lowly serpent to contribute to Adam and Eve abusing their free will, and disobeying God, believing they did not need him, and could walk on their own. – Genesis 3:1-6; Job 1-2.

God removed the rebellious Adam and Eve from the Garden of Eden. (Gen. 3:23-24) The first human couple had children, but they all grew old and eventually died. (Gen. 3:19; Rom. 5:12), just as the animals died. – Ecclesiastes 3:18-20

Genesis 6:5 (AT) tells us just before the flood of Noah, that "the wickedness of man on earth was great, and the whole bent of his thinking was never anything but evil." After the flood, God said of man, "the bent of man's mind may be evil from his very youth." (Gen 8:21, AT) Jeremiah 10:23 tells us "that it is not in man who walks to direct his steps." Jeremiah 17:9 tells us that "The heart is deceitful above all things, and desperately sick; who can understand it?" Yes, the man was not designed to walk on his own. However, the man was also not designed with absolute free will, but free will under the sovereignty of his Creator. The imperfect man is mentally bent toward wickedness, fleshly desires, to which Satan has set up this world, so it caters to the fallen flesh of imperfect humans. The apostle John tells us, "For all that is in the world, the desires of the flesh and the desires of the eyes and pride of life, is not from the Father but is from the world." – 1 John 2:16.

Getting back to Genesis 1:27 that says, "God created man in his own image, in the image of God he created him; male and female he created them," which means that man is born with a moral nature, which creates within him a conscience that reflects God's moral values. (Rom 2:14-15) It acts as a moral law within all imperfect humans but even more so, those who have trained the conscience with God's Word. However, it has an opponent as fallen man also possesses the "law of sin," 'missing the mark of perfection,' the natural desire toward wickedness. Listen to the internal battle of the apostle Paul. – Romans 6:12; 7:22-23.

Romans 7:21-24 English Standard Version (ESV)

21 So I find it to be a law that when I want to do right, evil lies close at hand. **22** For I delight in the law of God, in my inner being, **23** but I see in my members another law waging war against the law of my mind and making me captive to the law of sin that dwells in my members. **24** Wretched man that I am! Who will deliver me from this body of death?

However, there is hope,

Romans 7:25 English Standard Version (ESV)

25 Thanks be to God through Jesus Christ our Lord! So then, I myself serve the law of God with my mind, but with my flesh I serve the law of sin.

Yes, even imperfect man and woman have a conscience that reflects God's moral values. Therefore, when we hear of such things as ones being tortured, it is repugnant to us. Even if the person has committed some heinous crime, it is still sickening and abhorrent to the human mind, which reflects God's moral values on a small scale in our human imperfection. Therefore, we can only wonder how God, who has perfect moral values, would view the idea of torturing humans for an eternity, which is what the hellfire doctrine teaches.

Jeremiah 7:31 English Standard Version (ESV)

³¹ And they have built the high places of Topheth, which is in the Valley of the Son of Hinnom, to burn their sons and their daughters in the fire, which I did not command, nor did it come into my mind.

Imagine if we can, we have come home to find that our husband has inserted a pipe up the rectum of our 17-year-old daughter, with it coming out her mouth. He has her over a fire and is slowly cooking her alive. He has the fire set, so it will burn her very slowly, lasting days. He says that he is tired of her sinful actions, and she must pay for her rebellious spirit. How would our Christian conscience take that scene, would we simply set our purse down, and start helping him turn her on the thin rod on which she is impaled for roasting over the fire? Would we have no feeling as she screams out in agony? How do we place a loving and just God in such a light, when we only have a fraction of his moral values, and know that this scene would be so shocking and hurtful, it is unthinkable. Likely, as the reader started this paragraph, the language of even saying such things was so revolting that we have questioned why we even bought such a book. Keep in mind, it is our God given conscience that made us feel that way.

Regardless of this hypothetical daughter's sinful nature, and her rebellious spirit, a parent's heart would be torn in two. The disdain for the husband, the one who applied the torture, would be unbearable. The love of God is merciful and has the feeling of sympathy. A loving father may choose to punish his child but never torture. In fact, the United States will not allow any form of capital punishment (i.e., death penalty) that includes any pain and suffering. This is true, even when they are executing people for the vilest crimes.

Nevertheless, much of Christianity teaches that God is a torturer, and his form of justice is to exceed the crime, because he is vindictive, as a human rejected his sovereignty, so he burns this one alive, in an eternal hellfire. If a child refused to follow the rules of the house, would we kick her out, or would we burn her slowly over a fiery pit in the backyard? Which is more just, to kick a person out of eternal life (annihilationism), or to torturously burn them alive for an eternity. Who would create a torture chamber, and see that as justice? Would this be one who is repeatedly described as the epitome of love, justice, mercy, kindness, and wisdom?

1 John 4:8 English Standard Version (ESV)

[8] Anyone who does not love does not know God, because God is love.

Unreasonable Doctrine?

Does the above almighty being inflict eternal torture on a person, who has only sinned for 70 years? Does this sound like a person that deserves to be loved? Did not Adolf Hitler do the same thing to the Jews and Christians? Even if a human sinned every day of an 80-year lifetime grievously, would eternal fiery torment be a just punishment? Hardly! It would be unjust to God, who already told us how to view justice when he said an eye for an eye, a life for a life.

Deuteronomy 32:4 English Standard Version (ESV)

4 "The Rock, his work is perfect,

for all his ways are justice.

A God of faithfulness and without iniquity,

just and upright is he.

What Does Deuteronomy 32:4 Mean?

God's justice, like every other aspect of his unparalleled personality, is perfect, not lacking in anything. Every time God expresses his justice, it is flawless, never too lenient and never too harsh.

Holman Old Testament Commentary

32:1-4. Although the words of Moses in his song were designed to testify against Israel's coming defections, the true subject of the song was the greatness of our God. Once convicted of their sin, Israel would be brought back to God not by the failure of their idols but by the supreme faithfulness and beauty of the Rock of Israel, a God who does no wrong.[53]

New American Commentary

32:3-4 There clearly is a subject shift in v. 3, where Moses appears as a character witness on the Lord's behalf. Also addressing the heavens and the earth, he extols the Lord's greatness, especially by the public proclamation of his name, that is, of his reputation (v. 3; cf. Exod 33:19; 34:5-6). The expected result was that all who heard should ascribe greatness ("praise") to God. Knowledge of God can lead to no other response than to acknowledge his might. Specific expressions of his power are his identification as "the Rock" (haṣṣûr; cf. vv. 15, 18, 30; Hab 1:12), the foundation and fortress (cf. Pss 31:3; 62:7; 71:3; 89:26; 95:1; Isa 30:29) whose works are upright (thus tāmîm, "having integrity") and whose ways are characterized by justice (mišpāṭ, "rectitude"; cf. Gen 18:25; Job 40:8; Pss 111:7; 119:149). In the context of self-defense these

---

[53] Anders, Max; McIntosh, Doug, *Deuteronomy*, Holman Old Testament Commentary (Nashville: Broadman & Holman Publishers, 2002), 359-360.

attributes speak most particularly to the Lord's own character. Thus he is also faithful in the sense that he is dependable (ʾĕmûnâ; cf. Pss 88:11; 89:2–3, 6, 9; Isa 25:1; Hos 2:19), devoid of any hint of injustice (ʾên ʿāwel), a God who is righteous and just in all he does (v. 4b). These descriptions are especially apropos in a legal setting in which the reputation of the Lord may be under attack as he himself proceeds to level charges of impropriety against his covenant partner Israel.[54]

The main thoughts here, which apply to our discussion is, "God does no wrong," a God "devoid of any hint of injustice (ʾên ʿāwel), a God, who is righteous and just in all he does (v. 4b)."

Tsadaq, "to be righteous, be in the right, be justified, be just." This verb, which occurs fewer than 40 times in biblical Hebrew, is derived from the noun tsedeq. The basic meaning of tsadaq is "to be righteous." It is a legal term which involves the whole process of justice. God "is righteous" in all of His relations ..."[55]

[54] Eugene H. Merrill, *Deuteronomy*, vol. 4, The New American Commentary (Nashville: Broadman & Holman Publishers, 1994), 410.

[55] W. E. Vine, Merrill F. Unger, and William White Jr., *Vine's Complete Expository Dictionary of Old and New Testament Words* (Nashville, TN: T. Nelson, 1996), 205.

Now, let us look at the Son of God, and his perception of retribution.

Matthew 5:38-42 English Standard Version (ESV)

38 "You have heard that it was said, 'An eye for an eye and a tooth for a tooth.'39 But I say to you, Do not resist the one who is evil. But if anyone slaps you on the right cheek, turn to him the other also. 40 And if anyone would sue you and take your tunic, let him have your cloak as well. 41 And if anyone forces you to go one mile, go with him two miles. 42 Give to the one who begs from you, and do not refuse the one who would borrow from you.

What Did Jesus Mean?

Holman New Testament Commentary

5:38–42. As many people do today, the scribes and Pharisees of Jesus' day must have taken the "eye for an eye" passages (Exod. 21:24; Lev. 24:19–20; Deut. 19:21) as justification for hurting others at least as badly as they had been hurt. The law was not given to exact revenge, but to legislate justice. Breaking the law has consequences, but personal vengeance has no place. These passages have often been wrongly taken as a minimum guideline for retaliation. What Jesus clarifies is that they were always intended as a maximum or a ceiling for retaliation, and that mercy was always an acceptable intention underlying these laws.

For the kingdom servant, legalistically "letting the punishment fit the crime" and insisting upon a "pound of flesh" falls short. We must actually consider blessing the repentant criminal. Mercy (withholding deserved punishment) and grace (giving undeserved gifts) are legitimate norms of conduct.

The **one mile** (5:41) refers to the practice of the Roman soldiers requiring civilians to carry their burden for one mile. By Roman law, the soldier could require no more than one mile of a single porter, but Jesus' kingdom servants (in representing the gracious spirit of their king) are to go beyond what is required of them.[56]

New American Commentary

5:38–42 Jesus next alludes to Exod 21:24 and Deut. 19:21. Again, he formally abrogates an Old Testament command in order to intensify and internalize its application. This law originally prohibited the formal exaction of an overly severe punishment that did not fit a crime as well as informal, self-appointed vigilante action. Now Jesus teaches the

---

[56] Stuart K. Weber, *Matthew*, vol. 1, Holman New Testament Commentary (Nashville, TN: Broadman & Holman Publishers, 2000), 69.

principle that Christian kindness should transcend even straightforward tit-for-tat retribution. None of the commands of vv. 39–42 can easily be considered absolute; all must be read against the historical background of first-century Judaism. Nevertheless, in light of prevailing ethical thought Jesus contrasts radically with most others of his day in stressing the need to decisively break the natural chain of evil action and reaction that characterizes human relationships.

Antistēnai ("resist") in v. 39 was often used in a legal context (cf. Isa 50:8) and in light of v. 40 is probably to be taken that way here. Jesus' teaching then parallels 1 Cor 6:7 against not taking fellow believers to court, though it could be translated somewhat more broadly as "do not take revenge on someone who wrongs you" (GNB). We must nevertheless definitely resist evil in certain contexts (cf. Jas 4:7; 1 Pet 5:9). Striking a person on the right cheek suggests a backhanded slap from a typically right-handed aggressor and was a characteristic Jewish form of insult. Jesus tells us not to trade such insults even if it means receiving more. In no sense does v. 39 require Christians to subject themselves or others to physical danger or abuse, nor does it bear directly on the pacifism-just war debate. Verse 40 is clearly limited to a legal context. One must be willing to give as collateral an outer garment—more than what the law could require, which was merely an inner garment (cf. Exod 22:26–27). *Coat* and *shirt* reflect contemporary parallels to "cloak" and "tunic," though both of the latter looked more like long robes. Verse 41 continues the legal motif by referring to Roman conscription of private citizens to help carry military equipment for soldiers as they traveled.

Each of these commands requires Jesus' followers to act more generously than what the letter of the law demanded. "Going the extra mile" has rightly become a proverbial expression and captures the essence of all of Jesus' illustrations. Not only must disciples reject all behavior motivated only by a desire for retaliation, but they also must positively work for the good of those with whom they would otherwise be at odds. In v. 42 Jesus calls his followers to give to those who ask and not turn from those who would borrow. He presumes that the needs are genuine and commands us not to ignore them, but he does not specifically mandate how best we can help. As Augustine rightly noted, the text says "give to everyone that asks," not "give everything to him that asks" (*De Sermone Domine en Monte* 67). Compare Jesus' response to the request made of him in Luke 12:13–15. It is also crucial to note that "a willingness to forego one's personal rights, and to allow oneself to be insulted and imposed upon, is not incompatible with a firm stand for matters of principle and for the rights of others (cf. Paul's attitude in Acts 16:37; 22:25; 25:8–12)." Verses 39–42 thus comprise a "focal instance" of nonretaliation; specific, extreme commands attract our attention to a key ethical theme that must be variously applied as circumstances change.[57]

If the above are examples of how the Father and the Son see justice, retaliation, and retribution, it would clearly be injustice to torment someone in a pit of fire eternally, for a limited number of sins that was committed over a 70-80 year period.

There is only one person, who knows what happens after death, and it is God. He made it all too clear as to what happens to humans at death.

Ecclesiastes 3:19-20 English Standard Version (ESV)

19 For what happens to the children of man and what happens to the beasts is the same; as one dies, so dies the other. They all have the same breath, and man has no advantage over the beasts, for all is vanity. **20** All go to one place. All are from the dust, and to dust all return.

These verses have no mention of some eternal fiery torment. Humans simply return to the dust

---

[57] Craig Blomberg, *Matthew*, vol. 22, The New American Commentary (Nashville: Broadman & Holman Publishers, 1992), 113–114.

from which they came, no longer in existence, when they die. Some will receive a resurrection from the dead, other will simply remain dead forever.

If a person is to feel the torment of eternal hellfire, they have to be conscious. However, God inspired Solomon to write, "Yes, the living know they are going to die, but the dead know nothing. They have no further reward; they are completely forgotten." (Eccles 9:5) Based on this, it is impossible for those that have died, who "know nothing," to have knowledge of the anguishes of hellfire.

Dangerous Doctrine?

Some Christians would actually make the statement that 'the doctrine of hellfire is useful.' Why would they say that? They believe that it helps deter the Christian from sinning. Well, the same thing is believed about the death penalty for capital murder. Are not the United States prisons filled with death row inmates? In fact, the prison system is filled with all kinds of Christians, committing any number of different crimes. The truth is, the hellfire doctrine is actually harmful. If a person accepts that God tortures people for eternity, for sinning a mere 70-80 years, will they not view humans torturing humans as acceptable. Did not the Catholic Church torture Christians during the Inquisitions for simply disobeying the church? Yes, they burned them at the stake, stretched them on a rack,[58] until their bones broke, and beat them relentlessly.

If hellfire is so unreasonable logically, why do so many Christians, who claim to have the mind of Christ, accept such cruelty from their loving God? "Mind control (also known as brainwashing, coercive persuasion, thought control, or thought reform) is an indoctrination process that results in "an impairment of autonomy, an inability to think

---

[58] The rack is a torture device consisting of a rectangular, usually wooden frame, slightly raised from the ground, with a roller at one or both ends. The victim's ankles are fastened to one roller and the wrists are chained to the other. As the interrogation progresses, a handle and ratchet attached to the top roller are used to very gradually stepwise increase the tension on the chains, inducing excruciating pain. By means of pulleys and levers this roller could be rotated on its own axis, thus straining the ropes until the sufferer's joints were dislocated and eventually separated. Additionally, if muscle fibres are stretched excessively, they lose their ability to contract, rendering them ineffective.

One gruesome aspect of being stretched too far on the rack is the loud popping noises made by snapping cartilage, ligaments or bones. One powerful method for putting pressure upon prisoners was to force them to watch someone else being subjected to the rack. Confining the prisoner on the rack enabled further tortures to be simultaneously applied, typically including burning the flanks with hot torches or candles or using pincers made with specially roughened grips to tear out the nails of the fingers and toes.-- http://en.wikipedia.org/wiki/Rack_(torture)

independently, and a disruption of beliefs and affiliations. In this context, brainwashing refers to the involuntary reeducation of basic beliefs and values"[59] The term has been applied to any tactic, psychological or otherwise, which can be seen as subverting an individual's sense of control over their own thinking, behavior, emotions or decision making."[60] Yes, these ones were raised in ultra-religious households, where they were taught the hellfire doctrine from childhood, up unto their adult years, so it is a deeply ingrain belief.

Keep in mind that after Adam sinned. Imperfect humans had and have had a natural inclination toward sin. It bears repeating again, Genesis 6:5 (AT) tells us just before the flood of Noah, that "the wickedness of man on earth was great, and the whole bent of his thinking was never anything but evil." After the flood, God said of man, "the bent of man's mind may be evil from his very youth." (Gen 8:21, AT) Jeremiah 10:23 tells us "that it is not in man who walks to direct his steps." Jeremiah 17:9 tells us that "The heart is deceitful above all things, and desperately sick; who can understand it?" Yes, man naturally leans toward bad.

---

[59] Kowal, D. M. (2000). Brainwashing. In A. E. Kazdin (Ed.) , Encyclopedia of psychology, Vol. 1 (pp. 463-464). American Psychological Association.
[60]

http://en.wikipedia.org/wiki/Brain_washing#cite_note-1

What is the Punishment for Sin?

If the hellfire doctrine does not exist, what is the punishment for sin? What is Adam's punishment for rejecting God, what is the rest of humanities punishment for rejecting the Gospel? What was Adam told would happen, if he sinned? He was told, "for in the day that you eat of it the tree of knowledge] you shall surely die." (Gen 2:17) What happened to Adam? God told him, "By the sweat of your face you shall eat bread, till you return to the ground, for out of it you were taken; for you are dust, and to dust you shall return." (Gen. 3:19) What did Paul say was the punishment for sin? "The wages of sin is death." (Rom. 6:23) Life was and is a gift from God. If we reject God, if we willfully, sin unrepentantly, the gift is taken away, and we die.

The same Christians who have been programmed to accept the contradiction of a loving God, who tortures humans forever, would actually ask, 'how is that just, because everyone dies?' It is true that we all die. Why? Paul tells us, "sin came into the world through one man [Adam], and death through sin, and so death spread to all men because all sinned." We are all sinners.

If we all are sinners, and we all die, what is the point in trying to live a Christlike life? Is it true justice, if the one who is attempting to live a virtuous life, should die, just as the wicked man dies? However, this is irrational thinking, and some things are being left out of the formula of justice.

While both die, the righteous one will receive a resurrection, with the hope of eternal life. We see that Jesus 'gave his life as a ransom for many' (Matt. 20:28). We see that "all who are in the tombs will hear [the] voice [of Jesus] and come out, those who have done good to the resurrection of life, and those who have done evil to the resurrection of judgment." (John 5:28-29) We are told, "that there is going to be a resurrection, both of the righteous and the unrighteous." – Acts 24:15

Romans 5:18-21 English Standard Version (ESV)

¹⁸ Therefore, as one trespass led to condemnation for all men, so one act of righteousness leads to justification and life for all men. ¹⁹ For as by the one man's disobedience the many were made sinners, so by the one man's obedience the many will be made righteous. ²⁰ Now the law came in to increase the trespass, but where sin increased, grace abounded all the more, ²¹ so that, as sin reigned in death, grace also might reign through righteousness leading to eternal life through Jesus Christ our Lord.

Righteous Receive the Resurrection of Life

The wages of sin is death, and wages of willful unrepentant sin is eternal death (Heb. 6:4-6; 10:26-31), never being resurrected, as Paul said, "will suffer the punishment of eternal destruction." (2 Thess. 1:9) It is true that when we die, we no longer exist, except in the memory of God, as dead is

136

dead. However, as we are seeing here, the righteous will receive a resurrection. Even those in the Old Testament had a hope for something better, as Job's words clearly demonstrate,

Job 14:13-15 English Standard Version (ESV)

¹³ Oh that you would hide me in Sheol,

that you would conceal me until your wrath be past,

that you would appoint me a set time, and remember me!

¹⁴ **If a man dies, shall he live again?**

All the days of my service I would wait,

till my renewal should come.

¹⁵ **You would call, and I would answer you;**

you would long for the work of your hands.[61]

The righteous man Job believed that his remaining faithful to God, would result in God remember him after he had died, and one day, he would be resurrected. Jesus himself, speaking to a Jewish audience, confirmed the hope that the Israelites had been carrying for 2,000 years,

---

[61] This led him to consider the doctrine of resurrection and to wonder if it would be best for him to die and thus rest until the day when the dead rise (14:13–17). – David S. Dockery et al., *Holman Bible Handbook* (Nashville, TN: Holman Bible Publishers, 1992), 316.

John 5:28-29 English Standard Version (ESV)

28 Do not marvel at this, for an hour is coming when all who are in the tombs will hear his voice **29** and come out, those who have done good to the resurrection of life, and those who have done evil to the resurrection of judgment.

When Jesus returns, he will bring many angels, and wipe out the wicked. However, the righteous will not be destroyed, and the righteous prior to Jesus first coming back in the first century, will receive a resurrection. The unrighteous, which had never had the opportunity to know God, will also be resurrected for a chance to hear the Good News, and then, they will be judged on what they do during the millennial reign of Christ. Acts 24:15) Therefore, the punishment for sin is death, the punishment for those, who "keep on sinning deliberately after receiving the knowledge of the truth, there no longer remains a sacrifice for sins," i.e., eternal death. However, "there will be a resurrection of both the just and the unjust [i.e., those who never heard the Good News]." – Acts 24:15

Life on Earth under God's Kingdom

Isaiah 65:21-23 Updated American Standard Version (UASV)

21 They shall build houses and inhabit them;
   they shall plant vineyards and eat their fruit.
22 They shall not build and another inhabit;
   they shall not plant and another eat;

for like the days of a tree will the days of my people be,

    and the work of their hands my chosen ones will enjoy to the full.
23 They shall not labor in vain

    or bear children for calamity,
for they are the seed**62** made up of those blessed by Jehovah,,

    and their descendants with them.

On this, the Holman Old Testament Commentary says, "The injustices of life would disappear. Long life would be the rule for God's people, death at a hundred being like an infant's death that could only be explained as the death of a sinner. All of God's people would live to a ripe old age and enjoy the fruits of their life. The age of Messiah would clearly have dawned (cp. 11:6–9). No longer would people lose their property and crops to foreign invaders. Each of God's faithful people would enjoy the works of their hands. Labor would be rewarded in the field and in the birth place. Every newborn would escape the "horror of sudden disaster" (author's translation; NIV, misfortune). Curses would disappear. Every generation would be blessed by God."**63**

---

62 I.e., *offspring*

63 Anders, Max; Butler, Trent (2002-04-01). Holman Old Testament Commentary - Isaiah (p. 374). B&H Publishing. Kindle Edition.

Revelation 21:3-4 Updated American Standard Version (UASV)

³ And I heard a loud voice from the throne, saying, "Behold, the tabernacle of God is among men, and he will dwell[64] among them, and they shall be his people,[65] and God himself will be among them,[66] ⁴ and he will wipe away every tear from their eyes, and death shall be no more, neither shall there be mourning, nor crying, nor pain anymore, for the former things, have passed away."

"[God] will wipe away every tear from their eyes." (21:4) These are not tears of joy but rather tears that were the result of pain, suffering, old age, the loss of loved ones, and death. The Father will not only wipe away these tears of sorrow from our eyes but, he will remove them permanently forever, as he will have removed all that would ever lead to such tears, i.e., the removal of the *causes*.

"Death shall be no more." (21:4) Certainly, the enemy death has brought about more unwanted tears than anything else. After the thousand year reign of Christ, Satan will be released from the abyss for a while, succeeding to mislead many more. After that, those who have remained faithful will have the grip of death removed forever. The Father will remove the real cause of death; that is, the inherited

---

[64] Lit *he will tabernacle*

[65] Some mss *peoples*

[66] One early ms and be *their God*

sin from Adam. (Rom. 5:12) "The last enemy that will be abolished is death." (1 Cor. 15:26) Those who were faithful through the Great Tribulation, Armageddon, the Millennium, and the release of Satan for a little while will live for an eternity in a paradise earth, in human perfection, just as God had originally intended.

"Neither shall there be ... pain anymore." (21:4) The type of pain that is spoken of being removed here is the physical, mental, and emotional, which was brought on by the sin of Adam and the inherited imperfection that resulted after that. It will be no more.

This new life without tears, pain, mourning, crying, and death will certainly be a reality for those with a heavenly hope as they rule with Christ in heaven but also for those with an earthly hope, which is who is being spoken of here specifically. Notice that all of this was introduced with the words **"the tabernacle of God is among men."** (21:3) We know that men live here on earth. Moreover, the context is describing the renewed earth where **"death shall be no more."** This is referring the world where death had existed but will now be no more. Death has never existed in the spiritual heavens where the Father, the Son and the Holy Spirit, as well as the angels, live. However, for over six thousand years, death has existed here on the earth. Thus, the promises of Revelation 21:3-4 are meant specifically for those here on earth, which will be a restored or renewed earth.

The restored or renewed earth will be filled with people who fear God and sincerely love their neighbor. (Heb. 2:5; Lu 10:25-28.) The changes that take place as a result of God's heavenly Kingdom, namely, Jesus and his co-rulers, will be so weighty that the Bible speaks of "a new earth," i.e., a new faithful human society.

How is it that God "will dwell among them," that is among humankind after Armageddon? God would turn his attention to his people in the forthcoming renewed or restored earth, setting them free from sin and death. Then God will turn his attention to Satan the Devil, the god of this wicked world. The God of peace will abyss Satan for a thousand years, and then he will crush Satan by throwing him into the lake of fire. (2 Cor. 4:4; Rom. 16:20; Rev. 20:10, 14) After all of this, Jesus will hand the kingdom back over to the Father. (1 Cor. 15:28) After that, we do not know. However, we do know that more books will be opened during the millennium, where we will likely learn more.

OTHER BOOKS IN THIS SERIES

WHO IS THE ANTICHRIST

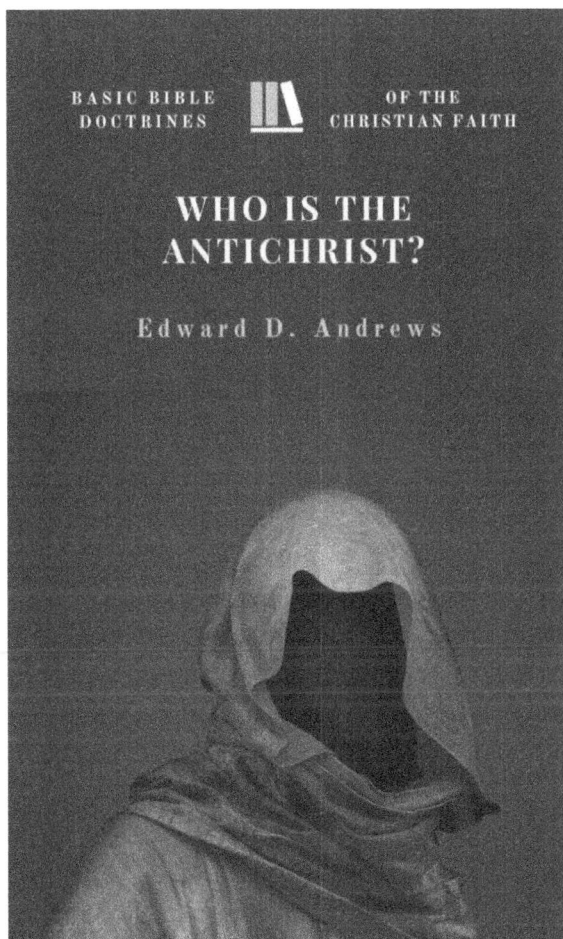

BASIC BIBLE
DOCTRINES

OF THE
CHRISTIAN FAITH

WHO IS THE
ANTICHRIST?

Edward D. Andrews

What Is Hell?

BASIC BIBLE
DOCTRINES

OF THE
CHRISTIAN FAITH

WHAT IS HELL?

Edward D. Andrews

BASIC BIBLE
DOCTRINES

OF THE
CHRISTIAN FAITH

The SECOND
COMING of CHRIST

Edward D. Andrews

BASIC BIBLE DOCTRINES   OF THE CHRISTIAN FAITH

EXPLAINING THE DOCTRINE OF MAN

Edward D. Andrews

BASIC BIBLE
DOCTRINES

OF THE
CHRISTIAN FAITH

EXPLAINING THE HOLY SPIRIT

Edward D. Andrews

Bibliography

Anders, Max, and Doug McIntosh. *Holman Old Testament Commentary - Deuteronomy (pp. 359-360).* . Nashville: B&H Publishing, 2009.

Brand, Chad, Charles Draper, and England Archie. *Holman Illustrated Bible Dictionary: Revised, Updated and Expanded.* Nashville, TN: Holman, 2003.

Bratcher, Robert G., and Howard Hatton. *A Handbook on the Revelation to John.* New York: United Bible Societies, 1993.

Bromiley, Geoffrey W., and Gerhard Friedrich. *Theological Dictionary of the New Testament, ed. Gerhard Kittel, vol. 4.* Grand Rapids, MI: Eerdmans, 1964-.

Bullinger, Ethelbert William. *Figures of Speech Used in the Bible.* London; New York: E. & J. B. Young & Co., 1898.

Elwell, Walter A. *Evangelical Dictionary of Theology (Second Edition).* Grand Rapids: Baker Academic, 2001.

Erickson, Milliard J. *Christian Theology.* Grand Rapids, MI: Baker Academic, 1998.

Gangel, Kenneth O. *Holman New Testament Commentary, vol. 4, John* . Nashville, TN: Broadman & Holman Publishers, 2000.

Kittel, Gerhard, Gerhard Friedrich, and Geoffrey William Bromiley. *Theological Dictionary of the New Testament.* Grand Rapids: Eerdmans, 1995, c1985.

Knight, George W. *The Pastoral Epistles: A Commentary on the Greek Text, New International Greek Testament Commentary.* Grand Rapids, MI; Carlisle, England: W.B. Eerdmans; Paternoster Press, 1992.

Lea, Thomas D. *Holman New Testament Commentary: Vol. 10, Hebrews, James.* Nashville, TN: Broadman & Holman Publishers, 1999.

McReynolds, Paul R. *Word Study: Greek-English.* Carol Stream: Tyndale House Publishers, 1999.

Mounce, William D. *Mounce's Complete Expository Dictionary of Old & New Testament Words.* Grand Rapids, MI: Zondervan, 2006.

Stein, Robert H. *A Basic Guide to Interpreting the Bible: Playing by the Rules.* Grand Rapids: Baker Books, 1994.

Thomas, Robert L. *Revelation 1-7: An Exegetical Commentary* . Chicago, IL: Moody Publishers, 1992.

—. *Revelation 8-22: An Exegetical Commentary* . Chicago, IL: Moody Publishers, 1995.

Towns, Elmer L. *Concise Bible Dictrines: Clear, Simple, and Easy-to-Understand Explanations of Bible Doctrines.* Chattanooga: AMG Publishers, 2006.

Vine, W E. *Vine's Expository Dictionary of Old and New Testament Words.* Nashville: Thomas Nelson, 1996.

Zodhiates, Spiros. *The Complete Word Study Dictionary: New Testament.* Chattanooga: AMG Publishers, 2000, c1992, c1993.

Zuck, Roy B. *Basic Bible Interpretation: A Prafctical Guide to Discovering Biblical Truth.* Colorado Springs: David C. Cook, 1991.